# Johnny Blackwell's
# POOR MAN'S
# CATALOG

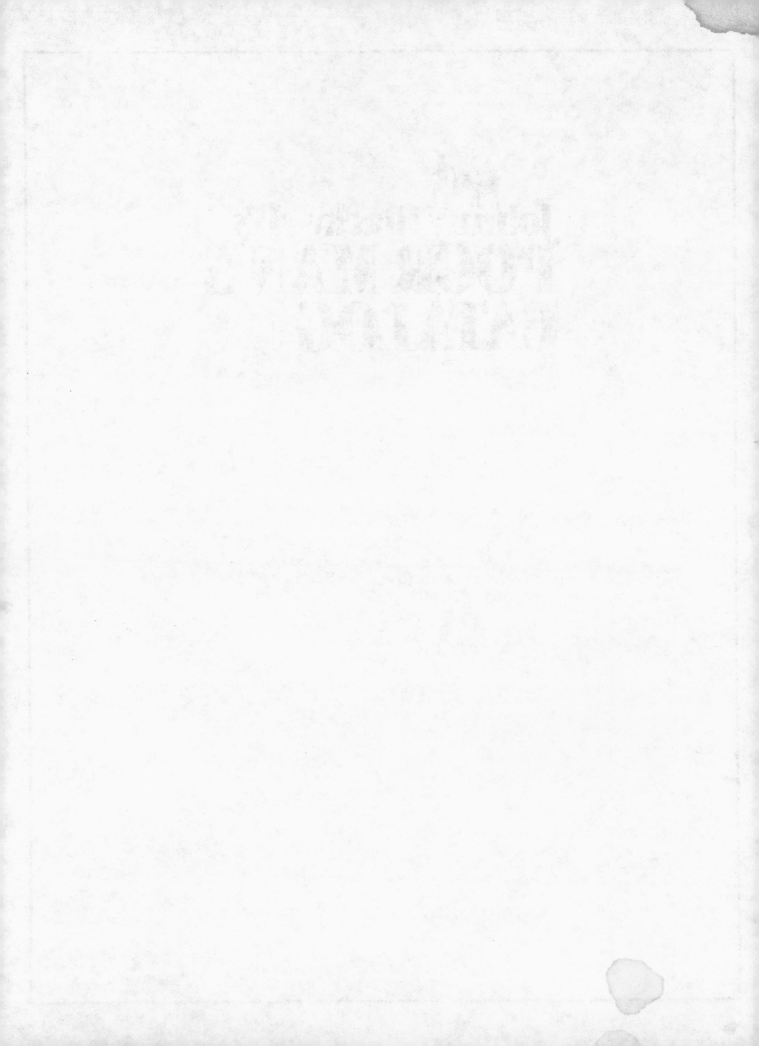

# Johnny Blackwell's
# POOR MAN'S CATALOG

**St. Martin's Press, New York**

To my wife and family...

without whose help this
book, our catalogs, and
the Poor Man would have
never been born.

Copyright © 1981 by Johnny Blackwell

All rights reserved.  For information, write:
St. Martin's Press, Inc., 175 Fifth Avenue,
New York, N.Y.  10010
Manufactured in the United States of America


Library of Congress Cataloging in Publication Data

Blackwell, Johnny.
    Johnny Blackwell's Poor Man's catalog.

    1.  Do-it-yourself work--Catalogs.  I.  Title.
II.  Title:  Poor Man's catalog.
TT153.7.B58          680          81-5793
ISBN  0-312-44464-8          AACR2
ISBN  0-312-44465-6 (pbk.)


10 9 8 7 6 5 4 3 2 1

First Edition

CONTENTS

I found the following little prayer in a rather odd place
(a gasoline service station), and I have no idea who should
get credit for writing it. But I'm sure they won't mind my
sharing it with you.

## THE MATURE PERSON'S PRAYER

Father, thou knowest I am growing older, please keep me from
becoming talkative and possessed with the idea that I must
express myself on every subject. Release me from the craving
to straighten out everyone's affairs. Keep my mind free from
the recital of endless detail. Seal my lips when I am in-
clined to tell of my aches and pains. Teach me the glorious
lesson that occasionally I may be wrong. Make me thoughtful
but not moody, helpful but not bossy.

With my vast store of wisdom and experience, it seems a pity
not to use it all, but thou knowest, Lord, that I want to
keep my friends.

Amen.

# INTRODUCTION

Dear Friends:

Welcome to <u>Johnny Blackwell's Poor Man's Catalog</u>. You will find in these pages a unique collection of money-saving ideas, plans, and projects--some old, others brand new, and all money-saving and useful. The idea behind this catalog is to show you some unusual ways to save both time and money. With our energy problems, inflation, and taxes, most folks are looking for ways to cut back and save bucks. The answer for more and more people is do-it-yourself. For many, it's no longer a do-it-yourself hobby--but a do-it-yourself necessity!

If you change the oil in your own car, paint a room, sew a bedspread, fix an appliance, or do any of a thousand other jobs that would cost you money, you are already a do-it-yourselfer. Over the years we have all been conditioned into thinking that when we need something, we have to go out and buy it. Now this is fine when the economy is perking along full steam and everyone is fat and happy. But should Hard Times drop on your head, you will find that those good old spending bucks just aren't spending as well anymore. During high inflation they have a rather nasty habit of shrinking. Worse yet, they grow fewer and farther between (known in Poor Man's lingo as scratching the bottom of the barrel). When this happens, we start thinking twice before parting with needed bucks for a product. If we really need the product, we could go into debt, we can do without, or we can build it ourselves. We really don't have much choice. Or do we? There is a way to avoid at least two of the choices just listed, and that is what the <u>Poor Man's Catalog</u> is all about.

While you cannot home-build every single product that is manufactured today, you certainly can give them a run for their money--especially in the time-saving, useful product area. Your home-built product will not be as flashy or as finished as the expensive commercial product, but in most cases it will work just as well, probably last longer, and surely cost much less. And, dear friends, when Hard Times are around, that "cost much less" can be very important. Ask anyone who was around during what is fondly remembered as the Great Depression. We are not saying that we should all go back and live in the past, although in some respects that might not be so bad. But we should all know that, come hard times, we can create and build our own products. And you may be surprised at the number and variety of products that can be home-built.

My family has been collecting, designing, and home-building useful products for years. None of us has any formal training or job-related experience in designing, construction, mechanics, or engineering. We started with a small basement shop in our home. It was pretty primitive by anyone's standards--a heavy-duty steel fire door purchased at a garage sale, along with some four-by-four oak lumber make up our workbench. We had several dozen assorted hand tools, a bench vise, and just three power tools: an electric drill, a portable power saw, and a small sabre saw. But, most important of all, we had motivation, a serious lack of extra bucks, and a whole lot of curiosity.

It all started innocently enough. My wife wanted a lighted signpost for the driveway with our name and house number. We had built our home in what was then a somewhat rural area, and a driveway sign would make it easier for folks to find us. So I built one that could be wired into our lamppost and would light up after dark. Some relatives and neighbors came over for a visit, saw our sign, and asked me to build one for them. As people told other people, it wasn't long before I was in the part-time sign-building business. We even started building small commercial signs for several small businesses. As one thing led to another, it wasn't long before I had more signs to build than time to build them. As I had to cut each letter and number out by hand, it seemed the faster I cut--the behinder I got! Something had to be done.

I started looking at engraving machine advertisements and sent away for sales literature on each one I could find. A large engraving machine would be just the thing to clear up my sign backlog as it would eliminate having to cut out each letter by hand. But, Wow! The prices on those things were well over a thousand dollars (and this was years ago). The few extra bucks that I was making on the signs just couldn't justify an outlay of that kind of bucks. With three growing kids and a new home mortgage, I didn't have the money anyway.

But we did have all of that sales literature with pictures and technical diagrams showing just how each engraving machine worked. Wasn't that nice! My oldest son and I spent most of that winter building and re-building our own version of a sign-engraving machine. We built it large enough to use a one-horsepower router for a power cutter as I was expecting the router as a Christmas gift. Our home-built engraving machine worked even better than we expected. Come spring, we were ready for business. Our new engraver not only cleared up our sign backlog, but made us enough extra money to allow us to buy a new high speed Dremel Moto tool. We rigged up a new power cutter arm for the engraver that would fit our new Dremel tool, and this allowed us to engrave plastic signs also. Now, in just hours, we could whip out either wood or plastic signs that would have taken days to cut out by hand.

Then one fine day, someone who had seen our sign-engraving machine in action said, "Why don't you try and sell the plans for your u-build engraving machine?" I was somewhat doubtful about this, as, after all, how many folks would be interested in a u-build engraver? Which goes to show you how little I knew. I went ahead and drew up the plans and instructions on how to build and operate our machine. With help from my family we wrote up our first sales letter. Then we built a little mimeograph machine from an old one-gallon paint can, and ran off copies of our machine plan and sales letter. Then I blew thirty-five bucks on a small classified advertisement in <u>Popular Mechanics</u> magazine, and crossed my fingers. I even said a little prayer as I mailed our ad and check, as my wife was all over me for throwing away thirty-five bucks!

Since it would be several months before our little advertisement was published, we spent the time designing and building a mini lathe for wood turning. We used a small sewing-machine motor to supply power and built a mini crossfeed so that it could be used like a metal lathe. We became so interested in wood turning that we went on to build a full-size wood turning lathe. We called it our sawhorse lathe because the complete lathe is built into a sawhorse. Once each project was completed and tested, we would draw up the plans and building instructions. My eldest son went on to design and build a simple faceplate lathe (no tailstock) which is still in use at a high school today.

After what seemed like a wait of three years, rather than just three months, our little classified ad was published. A slow trickle of cards and letters started to come into our post office box. Each respondent wanted more information on our u-build engraving machine, so we mailed them our mimeographed sales letter and hoped for the best. As the month progressed, more and more cards and letters came in. Before the end of the month we started getting our first orders. I quickly wrote up a new sales letter telling all about our new u-build lathes--the mini lathe, sawhorse lathe, and my son's faceplate lathe. This new sales letter was folded into each outgoing order of engraving machine plans. We hoped that this would result in new business. By the end of the month we had already processed well over 200 inquiries, and received orders for eleven plans, plus one re-order for a mini lathe plan. Things were indeed starting to look interesting.(Years later, I carefully went over our account books for this period and discovered that this little classified ad had paid for itself nineteen times over!) The following month as the orders started arriving regularly, I noticed that my wife had changed her tune. I heard no more about wasting thirty-five bucks.

By this time, I was convinced that there must be something to this plans by mail business. Using our profits, we placed more of those small classified ads in many national magazines. And I read everything I could find on the mail order business. For the next few years we worked at our new hobby during all our spare time. All three of our kids were still in school, and I did shift work which meant that someone was nearly always working in our basement shop/office. My wife would pick up the mail in the morning, sort out the orders from the inquiries, and record the order information. When our kids got home from school, our daughter would type shipping labels and file the orders. Then she and our youngest son would pull the plans ordered and fold them into mailing envelopes. Our oldest son would crank up our new duplicating machine (ordered from profits) and print whatever plans or sales letters needed to be reprinted to keep our stock up. When he wasn't busy with this, he helped me in the designing and building of projects. We would leave each other notes when I was working night shift. While all of this might sound greatly disorganized, it worked surprisingly well. On weekends we would all get together and discuss any problems that had cropped up. Everyone in the family received a percentage of whatever we made selling plans that month. Fifty percent always went back into the pot to pay for advertising and whatever supplies we needed. I can recommend this method to all parents as a great way to teach kids the value of money and how the free-enterprise system works. I honestly feel that our kids learned more from this "hands on" experience than any class taken in school (and even later in college.)

As time went on, we finally had enough plans and projects to consider printing a small catalog. We held a number of family discussions on this matter and finally decided to give it a try, even though the cost would completely wipe out our savings. While we wouldn't have to borrow, things would be very tight for a while. Again, each family member had to take responsibility for a certain part of the catalog. Since we couldn't afford commercial artwork, layout, or even typesetting, each of us had several important jobs. We were going to do everything but the actual printing in our home. I traded in our old manual typewriter for a good used electric model, and we built a much needed drafting table. I sincerely doubt if a lower-budget catalog has ever been produced. My daughter and I shared the artwork and the typing. We used little rub-on letters purchased from a stationery store to make headlines. My wife and youngest son did the pasteup, while our eldest son did the actual layout of the catalog. We decided to name our catalog the <u>Poor Man's Catalog</u>, not because you had to be poor to use it, but because we would be poor if you didn't!

Our catalog featured twenty-eight u-build projects and cost a quarter. We needed that quarter to help pay the printing costs. The entire project took us the best part of a year. After printing, the finished catalog looked like a home-designed effort, but we loved it. And apparently so did our customers. Still using just small classified advertisements, we sold out 10,000 copies of the catalog within six months. This encouraged us to try again, but rather than reprint the same catalog, we went to work on a series of new projects (including a few sent in by customers). The following year we produced our catalog #2, featuring fifty-seven u-build projects. We still produced the entire catalog at home, but since postage rates and printing had gone up, we charged fifty cents for this catalog. We marketed the catalog through the same small classified ads, along with about thirty small mail order dealers who had written to us and who wanted to sell the catalog on a percentage basis. Before long my wife had a collection of quarters and fifty-cent pieces that you wouldn't believe. She filled up quart mason jars with coins, and our bank teller would shudder when she came in the bank door.

By this time, folks all across the country were writing and sending ideas for new projects. Some the donors had actually built, others were just ideas. In some cases we purchased project plans that we thought would be of interest to our customers. Others would not accept anything and I suppose just wanted to show folks that they had built something worthwhile. Since we did our best to answer all letters, we made friends across the country and in a few cases carried on correspondence for years with folks we had never met. During all this time I had not been aware that some of the national magazines that we advertised in also published international editions. We started receiving inquiries for our catalogs from all over the world. Some from countries we had never even heard of before--so many, in fact, that my daughter took up stamp collecting. (I mentioned her stamp collecting later on a national TV show, and she received hundreds of letters from stamp collectors along with sample stamps. Thank you, kind people.) There is a story with one of these overseas letters that I just have to tell. And it really did happen. I have the proof, even if I didn't believe it at the time.

One Saturday morning I went to pick up our mail and noticed one of those tissue-thin overseas letters. This letter was from a gentleman in Africa. Although written in somewhat broken English, it was understandable. This gentleman had read one of my first small ads in one of the mechanics-type magazines that published international editions. This advertisement started with the headline "$$$$ MACHINE, reproduces, carves, engraves, metal, wood, etc." describing our u-build engraving machine. Somehow, this gentleman had misinterpreted my ad to read that I was in the international counterfeiting business. On four sheets of tissue-thin air mail stationery, he had written a complete plan of how he would trade me uncut diamonds in return for counterfeit U.S. dollars and counterfeit Ghana notes. He went into great detail as to postal drops, avoiding customs inspections, and security measures. He even offered to exchange samples! Now, I would be less than honest if I told you that I wasn't sorely tempted. I could just see those big sparklers, rolling in by the bag full. But then I got to thinking, how would I go about selling a batch of real, uncut diamonds? I could imagine dropping in on our local jewelry store for an evaluation of my stones, then trying to explain to the jeweler how I found them under my tomato plants. As soon as the word got out, I would have all my neighbors out ripping up

their lawns and gardens looking for diamonds. Kooks, nuts, and IRS agents
would start digging up my lawn and tearing my house down board by board,
looking for hidden diamonds. On second thought, the deal didn't look so
good after all. Besides, the stones were probably hotter than a wood
stove in February, and I would end up in the slammer for forty years. So
ended my brief international counterfeiting career. But, it was a nice
dream: Diamond Jim Poor Man!

Meanwhile, our little catalog business was booming along. We completely
sold out of the first and second printings of our Poor Man's Catalog
#2 (40,000 copies in all), and were hard at work on new projects for a
new catalog #3. We took our time with this one, as it would have a
whopping twenty-five pages and more than double the plans and projects.
With the help of one of our larger associates in New Jersey, we would
finally have typesetting and some commercial art layout. While our catalog still wasn't as slick and fancy as those produced by the big mail
order houses, it was at least starting to look respectable. It had taken
us over two years to go from catalog #2 to our new catalog #3, but we
felt that the end result was well worth the wait. Shortly after publishing #3, we got our first big break in the public news media. The
Washington Post Sunday magazine (Potomac) published a small article about
our family catalog business and gave our home address and phone number--
which was a big mistake. That Sunday morning our phone started ringing
at 6 AM. No one at the paper had informed us that the article would be
published, so we didn't know what was going on. We found out from one of
our early morning callers, who was more than happy to tell us all about
the story in the newspaper. By then, my entire family was up, and we ate
breakfast between phone calls. By 9 AM people had started to drop by and
our driveway was getting crowded with cars. By noon, when church let out,
we had folks parked in the driveway, on the lawn, and out into the
street. Meanwhile, the phone was still ringing off the hook. By mid-
afternoon we had folks from as far as southern Pennsylvania and northern
Virginia driving in just to say hello, and shoot the breeze. And, of
course, all wanted a catalog. My wife went through four gallons of iced
tea and at least four dozen soft drinks, plus all our cookies. But we
loved every minute of it and got to meet some wonderful folks. The next
day, the mail started coming in and we spent the next two weeks opening
envelopes and mailing catalogs.

Six months later we were still receiving inquiries for our catalog from that one small article. Needless to say, this taught me a big lesson about the public media. Namely, that you could mail out free catalogs with a press release, and stand a chance of getting some really good, FREE publicity. However, our associates in New Jersey came up with our next big break. They had also sent out press releases with sample catalogs. One day when arriving home from work about 5 PM, I received a phone call from Chicago. A very wonderful lady by the name of Janet Murray, of the Chicago Tribune, had seen and liked our catalog enough that she wanted to do a feature story on it. Sure enough, three weeks later on Sunday, November 27, 1977, the Poor Man's Catalog was featured in a half-page article in the Chicago Tribune. This time, our associates in New Jersey got the bulk of the mail, which poured in for four weeks and totaled thousands of inquiries. The story went out on the Tribune's wire service and soon other papers all over the country started carrying the story. Our new catalog had to go in for a quick second, and a third printing, for a total of over 70,000 catalogs.

All this publicity and excitement was just great, but it sure played hob with our family life. I was still working full-time, and our kids were still in school. There just didn't seem to be enough time in the day. Our little hobby was suddenly turning into a full-scale business. We were even starting to hear from libraries all over the world: Berlin, London, Tokyo, Madrid, Naples, Paris--it was hard to believe, all of this interest in a small family hobby. It was about time for me to do some heavy thinking on the matter. Did we really want to go into business full-time? Would it last, or was it all just a fluke? I had eighteen years in my job counting towards retirement. Could I give this up and take a chance on our catalog as a business? We held a family meeting and it was decided that we would pull in our horns for a bit, not do any advertising, and take our time and analyze the situation. So, for the next year we placed no advertising, and allowed things to calm down a bit. We did a lot of work on new plans, projects, and ideas. The volume of mail slowed down to a trickle and gave us plenty of time to work up new projects. I even started catching up on chores around the house.

In October 1978 we published a brand new Poor Man's Catalog #4. We had again more than doubled its size and number of u-build projects. We still

placed no advertising, but we mailed our brochures to all of our previous customers telling them about the brand new catalog. We rented
several mailing lists of names from some of the larger mail order
houses, and mailed our brochures to their customers. This direct mail
did quite well and we were ready to try it for the next year. Then, in
January 1979, I received a phone call from Popular Photography magazine,
who wanted more information on our new catalog and especially on our new
u-build photographic equipment section. They wanted to do a small article
for their March 1979 issue. I described how my eldest son had become interested in photography, how he had spent most of his savings for a good
camera, and how we decided to try and build some of the equipment that
he needed since it was so expensive. Then I described some of the equipment and the different methods we used to build it. After the article
was published, we heard from hundreds of amateur photographers all over
the country. Lots of these folks had done the same thing we had: built
their own equipment. Many sent beautiful photographs of their home-built
photo equipment. Some even went to the trouble to draw up step-by-step
plans of pieces of equipment they had built. What struck me as somewhat
unusual was that all these kind of folks wanted to share their ideas with
anyone who was interested in photography. And we learned a great deal
from them.

In early March, I received a totally unexpected phone call from a young
gentleman by the name of Mark Bowllan. Mr. Bowllan was a producer for a
local Baltimore TV show called "Evening Magazine." He explained that
someone had sent WJZ-TV 13 one of our new catalogs, and "Evening Magazine" was interested in doing a videotaped interview at our home. When
could we set up a date? Rather than give a definite date, I asked if I
could take his phone number and call him back. Now, my friends, it's one
thing to give an interview and get an article in a newspaper or magazine,
but it's something else again to get up in front of a TV camera with the
thought of thousands of people watching you. Just the thought gave me the
nervous shakes. I talked over this call with my family, and while we were
divided on the idea, my wife supported me in not rushing into the thing.
For one thing, she pointed out that our home is certainly not fancy or
large. And folks watching TV usually expected to see something special.
Secondly, we had long ago run out of room in our basement office/shop
and had stored, or given away, many of the projects we had built. What if

the TV people wanted to film everything in the catalog? Where in the
world could we put all of the stored projects, as we just didn't have
the room. Finally, we decided not to worry about it, and I would just
forget it. But we didn't count on Mr. Bowllan being a very stubborn fellow. He called again the following week, and I made an excuse and put
him off. Two weeks later he called again, and again I tried to make an
excuse, but he was way ahead of me. He realized that the big problem was
that I was just plain "chicken" and didn't want to get up in front of
any TV cameras. He explained how the interview would work, and that if I
made a goof it could be edited out with no problem. He made it sound like
fun, and very easy. So I finally agreed and a date was set.

On the following Saturday at 11 AM, a panelled truck with "Evening Magazine, Channel 13" painted on the sides, pulled into our driveway. This
immediately brought all the kids in the neighborhood to our house, and
we had a live audience before we even got started. We all pitched in to
help unload the big cameras, lights, extension cords, video cassettes,
sound recorders, and what seemed like 300 other parts of assorted gear.
It was decided to tape the first part of the interview in our dining
room, and the second part down in our basement shop/office. Once enough
electrical outlets were found to hook in all of the equipment, the
special lights were cut on. Immediately the room temperature shot up to
110 degrees. Boy, those lights are hot! And my galloping case of the
nervous shakes didn't help any. We finally got through the first part
of the interview with me showing copies of our first catalogs, our original u-build engraving machine, and assorted small projects. Each video
cassette ran for about fifteen minutes, and with re-takes, and closeups,
we ran through about four of them. Then we all moved downstairs for the
second part of the interview. And when I say "all" I mean my wife, three
kids, camera crew, at least forty-eight neighborhood kids, our little
Pekingese (who thought he should be in every shot), and myself. Along
with us went all the camera equipment, lights, cables, recorders, and
assorted equipment--all into a fourteen-by-twenty-foot room already
crowded with my workbench, shelves, desk, photocopy machine, our new
offset press, and my wife's washer and dryer.

Somehow, the TV producer sorted out all the parts and we got the second
part of the show on the road. My wife and daughter showed how we filled
orders, typed labels, and later filed the order forms. Our youngest son

started up our offset press and ran through a dry run for the camera. I
showed some of our printed plans, and explained a little about each one.
Then the producer asked me to show some current projects that we were
still working on. I showed a cotton candy machine made from a cake tin
that we were still working on, along with some experimental heating devices that we had designed and were still testing. One of these was a
small metal device, that we call a "Heat Booster" which fits over an
ordinary lightbulb and extracts heat from the bulb. I should have
stressed that this device was still experimental and not available on
the market, because later we heard from thousands of folks who wanted
more information on our Heat Booster. It was later decided that this device required just a little too much precision metal cutting for the av-
erage do-it-yourselfer, and we are looking for a manufacturer for it.

When the interview was finally over, I was astonished to learn that it
was already 6 PM! Our little interview had lasted seven hours, and used
a total of twelve complete video cassettes! All of this for about an
eight-minute segment on the "Evening Magazine" TV show.

On April 9th we were notified that our part of the show would be aired
on Tuesday, April 17th. By this time I had located a commercial mailing
house in nearby Columbia, Maryland, with whom we had reached an agree-
ment that they would handle our catalog mail inquiries and mail out our
catalogs. From our experiences with newspapers and magazines, we already
knew how easy it was to be swamped with mail. This time we would be
ready! Two days after the show was aired, the good people of Baltimore
did indeed swamp us with mail! The show had turned out beautifully. The
producer had dubbed in some crazy background music which seemed to fit
right in with the mood of the show. The videotape had been edited with
precision to show only the highlights, and my visible case of the galloping nervous shakes didn't show up on the screen. Friends later asked how
I had stayed so calm and collected. If they only knew! Three weeks after
the show, I received a phone call from the producer and after discussing
how well the show went over, he laid the big one on me! It seems that
"Evening Magazine," along with "PM Magazine," is a syndicated TV show.
It is seen in cities all across the country. Sometimes a locally taped
show is selected to be shown in all these cities on the same night. And
guess who got lucky? I about fainted! Our little segment would be seen

in cities from San Francisco, California, to Washington, D.C.  So, on
June 7, 1979, we got to watch the show all over again, only this time
from a Washington, D.C., station. One of Murphy's well-known laws is "If
anything can go wrong--it will!" And it did. We learned later that our
address was given in only five of the cities in which the show was seen
that night. It was left up to each local TV station to give our address
in case viewers wished to order our catalog. Worse yet, our address was
given as Baltimore, Maryland, rather than Highland, Maryland, as it
should have been. But they all did give the correct zip code for
Highland. Needless to say, this little error just about drove the main
Baltimore Post Office right up the walls! Even though our address had
been given in only five cities, the mail was arriving by the bagful!
And it just kept coming. Months later, we were still receiving mail for
our catalogs from this TV show. Over 160,000 catalog #4's were mailed to
wonderful folks all over the country.

An interesting offshoot from all of this free TV publicity was that a
young man in Washington, D.C., sent for one of our catalogs. Several
weeks later, he wrote to us and wanted an appointment. His name is
Raphael Sagalyn, and he is a literary agent. At our meeting, after showing him around our home and office/shop, he explained that one of the
large book publishing houses might be interested in publishing our Poor
Man's Catalog. Since we had never even considered our little catalog as
a book, we were somewhat shocked, but certainly interested. After several more meetings at which we discussed and worked up some new material,
our new agent presented this material and an outline of a brand new catalog to a New York publishing house. And, dear reader, you hold the results in your hands.

So what are we going to do now, since our Poor Man's Catalog has been
published as a book? Why, we are already hard at work on a brand new
Poor Woman's Catalog, what else!

                                                    J.S. Blackwell
                                                    THE POOR MAN

# Home Workshop

The power tools shown below are not available in <u>this</u> catalog. They are available in our self-published Poor Man's Catalog #5.

Gad! I wonder if my homeowners insurance covers this?

You've heard of a chicken in every pot? What we really need is an oilwell in every backyard!

# THE LAUGHING LANDLORD

After we married, my new wife and I spent a number of years enjoying the joys of apartment living. Like most young couples we couldn't afford any of the super-luxury apartments, so we did a lot of looking for low-cost apartments, something just as scarce then as now. We did finally locate one run-down apartment that the landlord laughingly called his economy apartment. If I would agree to fix up the place while living there, the landlord would knock off 25 percent from the rent. He agreed to pay for all materials used to patch up the place. As soon as we moved in I started learning just what the landlord had in mind when he said an "economy" apartment. Nothing worked! The john wouldn't flush, half the lights wouldn't work, and the kitchen sink was disconnected. And that wasn't the half of it, but the rent was at least reasonable. Our first few weeks in the apartment were a real ball, as you can imagine. But I did get a great deal of useful experience learning how to fix leaking faucets, plumbing, plaster, and painting. I also started a new collection of repair tools to add to my auto-repair assortment. I did take time out long enough to design my first workbench, which was really a workchest, a simple box-like affair that folded up and was easily stowed in a closet or under a bed. (This workchest was later redesigned into our Hobby Work Chest, shown above.) At the end of our first month, our laughing landlord called to collect the rent and inspect our work. When I handed him the bills for repair materials, he just handed them back and said we would settle up when all the repairs were complete. I should have smelled a rat, but being young, I took the man at his word.

So we spent the next happy month patching plaster, painting, and rewiring light switches in the apartment. I now had repair bills totaling over one hundred bucks and our little apartment was in pretty good shape. At the end of the month our laughing landlord was right on time to collect the rent. Again, I handed him the materials bills, and again he handed them back. I explained that the repairs were done and that it was time to settle up. He just laughed and said that now the apartment was fixed up, he would have to raise the rent. Rather than give him a shot in the nose, for which I was most tempted, I managed to control my temper and handed him the month's rent. The very next day, my wife went out apartment hunting while I drew on my newly acquired apartment re-pair skills to really work on that apartment. Our laughing landlord was going to get a real special remodeling job on that apartment before we moved out. By the end of the month we were long gone when our laughing landlord showed up to collect the rent. But he was the proud owner of the only apartment in town where the john flushed with steaming hot water, all of the light switches were installed backwards, with burned out bulbs in all of the fixtures, and when you turned on the water in the kitchen sink, the drain water poured out over your feet. I am sure that he got plenty of laughs when he tried to rent that apartment again. Especially when he walked into the living room and found the impressive, full sized, wall mural done on the ceiling. After all, how many land-lords can boast of a fifteen foot long cockroach, painted in living color on the ceiling? I wonder if he's still laughing? I am!

THE POOR MAN

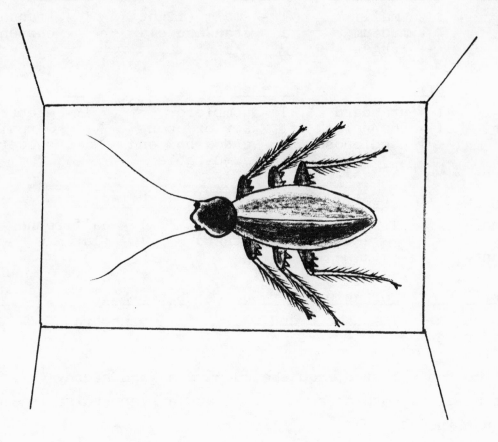

# BASIC TOOLS

I suppose I first started collecting tools as a teenager. My first car, a 1931 Model "A" Ford (previously owned by 400 other teenagers), required the use of a wide assortment of basic tools to keep running. Not because anything was wrong with the car, but because I kept fiddling with it. Over the years, going through at least a dozen old used cars, I picked up a mess of assorted screwdrivers, pliers, wrenches, sockets, and even spare parts. Know anyone who needs a '49 Ford waterpump?

Since every serious do-it-yourselfer must have some basic tools to get started, I have prepared a list of very basic tools for the new do-it-yourselfer. While I am sure that not everyone will agree with my list, all of the most basic repairs can be made with these tools. I might also pass on to the new do-it-yourselfer that I have found that it pays to buy good quality, brand name tools. Good quality tools will usually outlast the el-cheapo, no-name tools, ten to one. Plus you are less likely to get hurt using quality tools. Many el-cheapos will break under hard use.

| Screwdrivers | Phillips Head Screwdrivers | Hammer | Handsaw |
|---|---|---|---|
| 1 - small | 1 - small | 1 - small (light | 1 - standard |
| 1 - medium | 1 - medium | 1 - standard claw | carpenter |
| 1 - large | 1 - large | | |

| Hacksaw | Pliers | Wrenches | Soldering Gun |
|---|---|---|---|
| 1 - metal cutting | 1 - standard | 1 - complete set of open end & box end | 1 - electric acid & rosin core solder |
| | 1 - channelock | | |
| | 1 - needlenose | 1 - adjustable | |

| Allen wrenches | Steel Tape Measure | Files |
|---|---|---|
| 1 - set (good quality very important) | 1 - retractable (good quality important) | 1 - half round |
| | | 1 - flat |

| Electric Drill | Portable Power Saw | Sabre Saw | Vise |
|---|---|---|---|
| 1 - name brand with assorted drill bits | 1 - name brand | 1 - name brand | 1 - bench |

Along with the tools listed, you should have a good sturdy workbench. The workbench serves both as a work area and a place to store your tools when not in use.

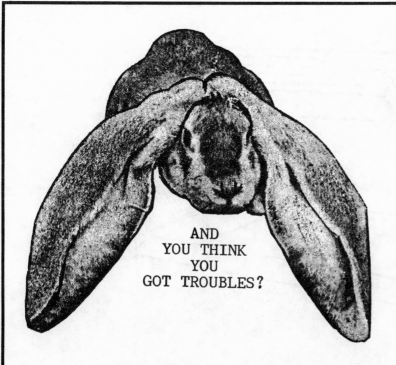

AND
YOU THINK
YOU
GOT TROUBLES?

## REPAIRING RESISTANCE WIRE

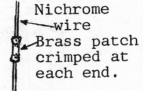

Nichrome wire

Brass patch crimped at each end.

Brass tube

Resistance or nichrome wire that has burned in half in an old toaster or electric heater can be repaired. Use a small length of brass tube cut from an empty ballpoint pen. Insert the burned-off ends of the wire into the tube and crimp them with pliers.

## POLITICIAN'S LAW

Promise them anything, but give them nothing in writing.

## POOR MAN'S SNEAKY SNAKE

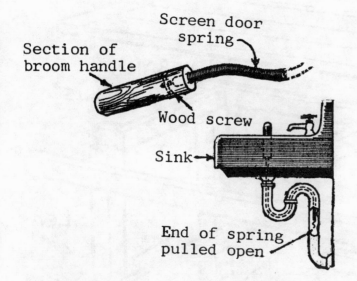

Screen door spring

Section of broom handle

Wood screw

Sink

End of spring pulled open

## DRILL PRESS MACHINING

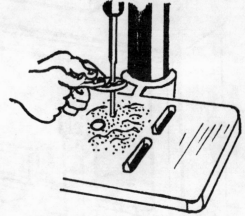

Build our simple little snake as shown above and you have an emergency drain cleaner. Since drains always seem to stop up only on weekends and holidays when no plumber is around, our Sneaky Snake could come in handy. Cut a 6" section of broom handle and drill out the center about 2" deep to accept a screen door spring. Pull one loop of spring out and screw a wood screw through handle and spring loop. At the other end of spring, pull open several loops for cleaning. Twist handle when using to clean drain.

Don't have a lathe? You can do a limited amount of metal machining using just a drill press. Chuck the rod firmly and spin at a relatively slow speed. Grasp the rod with a pair of pliers and, with a gentle pressure, turn down the diameter. The pliers will chew off extra metal while maintaining a perfect center. Finish with a file and emery cloth.

POOR MAN'S WORKBENCH

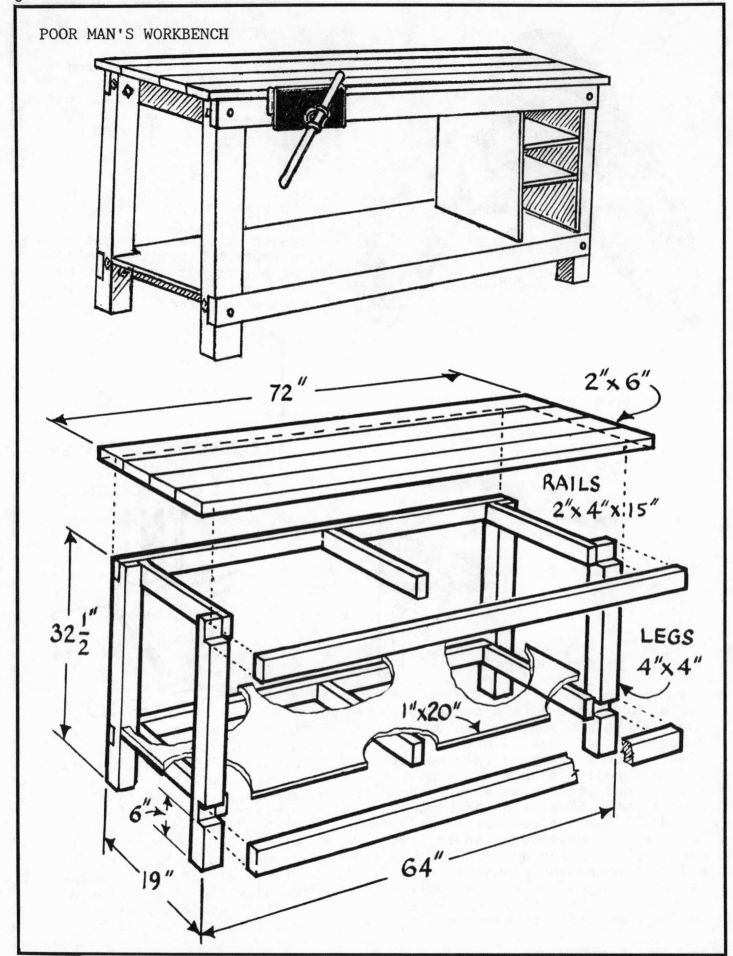

72"

2"x 6"

RAILS
2"x 4"x 15"

32 1/2"

LEGS
4"x 4"

1"x20"

6"

19"

64"

POOR MAN'S WORKBENCH continued

Your workbench will probably be the most important piece of equipment in your shop.
While limited in size to the space available
to you, it should be big enough to handle
most any size job, and strong enough to with-
stand much hammering and sawing. The workbench
plan shown here is an exact duplicate of my
own home workbench except for the bench top.
Where the plan calls for 2" X 6" wood planks,
my bench top is a heavy steel fire door found
by luck at a garage sale. I used only rough
cut oak lumber for the frame, but either fir
or hard maple would do. The frame is bolted
together with ¼" X 4" machine bolts. The
wooden bench top is installed using 3½"
(countersunk) flathead wood screws. If you
wish to install a woodworker's vise as shown,
a cutout (vise-size) must be made in the frame
before installing the bench top. Built according to this plan, your workbench should last
a lifetime.

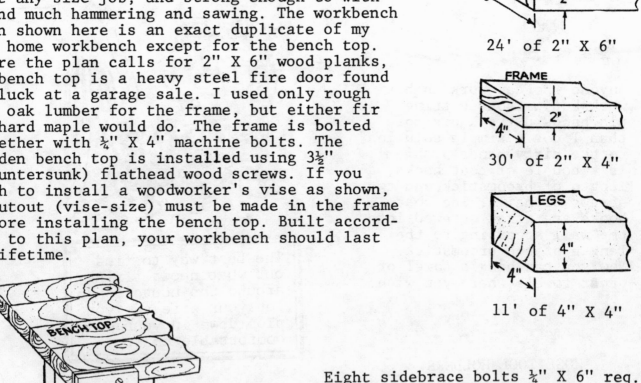

(MAIN PIECES ONLY)

**BENCH TOP**
6"  2"
24' of 2" X 6"

**FRAME**
4"  2"
30' of 2" X 4"

**LEGS**
4"  4"
11' of 4" X 4"

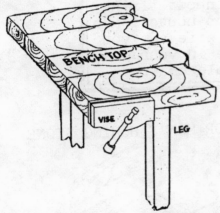

BENCH TOP

VISE       LEG

If the ends of the bench top are
extended far enough and reinforced
underneath, the woodworker's vise
can be installed at one end.

SHELVES

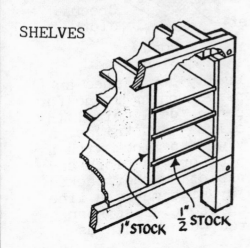

1" STOCK   1½" STOCK

Eight sidebrace bolts ¼" X 6" req.

**CORNER JOINT**

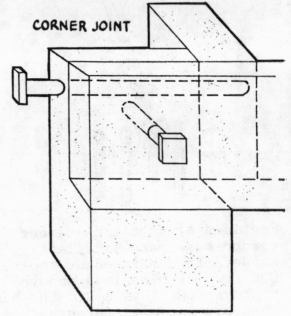

NOTE: The bolt holes are not located in the center of each piece,
but located so that bolts will
cross with 1" between each other
at joints.

## SHOP TOWEL HOLDER

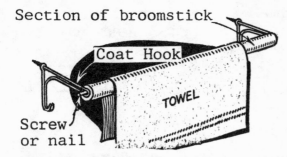

Anyone who can work in his
workshop without getting
his hands dirty knows more
than I do. A simple solution
to the dirty hands problem
is a couple of coat hooks, a
length of broomstick and two
screws or nails. The coat
hooks are first screwed into
the wall according to the
length of the broomstick.
Now you can hang a towel or
paper towels where you wish.

The best way to find
out what needs fixing
around the house is to
let your wife see you
plop down in your most
comfortable chair.

## HOSE TOOL HOLDERS

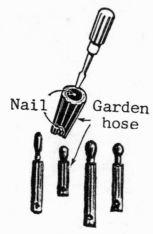

Sections of an old discarded
garden hose make excellent
holders for sharp-edged tools.
Cut each section long enough
to cover the tool up to the handle.
Then put one nail through the
bottom and one through one side of
the top to help attach to wall.

## POOR MAN'S HONING STONE

You really don't need an
expensive honing stone for
sharpening dull chisels,
plane irons and knives. A
heavy wooden block with a
strip of crocus cloth and
a strip of leather tacked
side-by-side makes a fine
honing stone. Just keep
covered when not in use.

## TOOL CABINETS AND STORAGE

Here is a simple add-a-unit method of constructing cabinets for tools and supplies. Start by building simple shelves, then just add on to the shelves as shown.

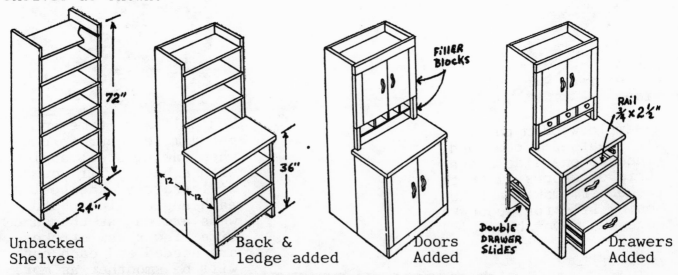

Unbacked Shelves — Back & ledge added — Doors Added — Drawers Added

## OVER THE WORKBENCH CABINET

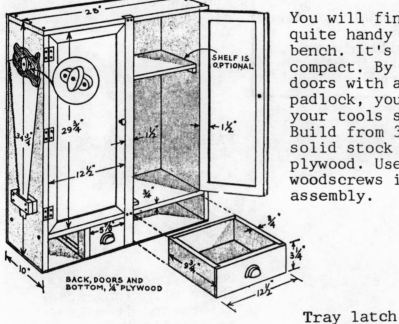

SHELF IS OPTIONAL

BACK, DOORS AND BOTTOM, ¼ PLYWOOD

You will find this cabinet quite handy over your workbench. It's commodious yet compact. By providing the doors with a hasp and padlock, you can keep your tools safe. Build from 3/4" solid stock or plywood. Use woodscrews in assembly.

DADO CUTS

TOOL RACKS

## PORTABLE TOOL BOX

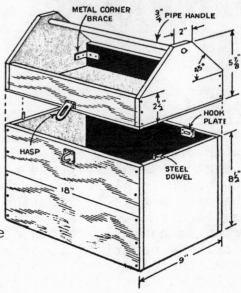

METAL CORNER BRACE — PIPE HANDLE — HOOK PLATE — HASP — STEEL DOWEL

Many times you will have to take your tools outside to do the job. This little portable tool box is just the ticket. Build from 3/4" plywood. Note that the detachable tray actually sits on top of the box leaving extra space for tools inside the box.

Tray latch Detail

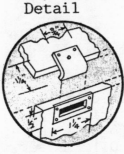

Two hook-and-plate sets are made and attached as shown on back of tray.

## POOR MAN'S HONING FILE

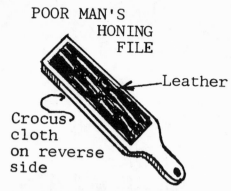

Leather

Crocus cloth on reverse side

A simple wooden paddle with leather tacked and glued to one side and a strip of crocus cloth to the other, makes a fine honing file for super-keen edges on mower blades.

## CUTTING STEEL ANGLES ACCURATELY

You will save time and get a more accurate cut when sawing steel angles with a hacksaw if you will start at the heel of each angle. Since both webs are cut at the same time, fewer saw strokes are needed and each cut will be smoother as more teeth are in contact with the angle.

### HANDYMAN'S LAW

The tool that you need to make an emergency repair will always have mysteriously disappeared.

## DRILL LUBRICATION

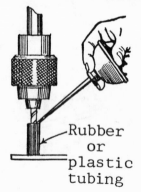

Rubber or plastic tubing

You can increase the life of high-speed drill bits many times over with proper lubrication. A short length of loose-fitting plastic or rubber hose placed over the drill in use, allows lubrication to be applied through the tubing. Oil that is normally thrown off the drill by centrifugal force drains down tubing directly to the work point where it does the most good.

## PAPER CLIP CONTACT

Lead wire

Bend a paper clip as shown with long nose pliers and it makes an excellent contact for small voltage jobs. Most of the bending is done on the long outer loop. The short loop must have spring action for firm contact with wire.

 *Don't throw me away when you're done. Me thinks I'll be a collector's item!*

## SAWHORSE TOOLBOX

For those folks with limited space, here are several ideas for space-saving workbenches.

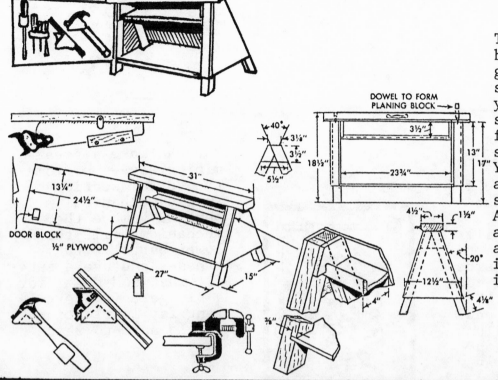

DOWEL TO FORM PLANING BLOCK

40°

3⅛"
3½"

18½"

5½"

31"

13¼"

24½"

DOOR BLOCK
½" PLYWOOD

27"

15"

⅜"

3½"

23¾"

13"

17"

4½"

1½"

20°

12½"

4⅛"

This little saw-horse toolbox can give you both space to store your tools and a solid work surface for your hammering, sawing, and planing. You will have to add tool racks to suit your own tools. Add a shoulder strap and it's portable, allowing you to take it where the work is.

## FOLD-DOWN WORKBENCH

Perfect for a garage or carport. Just build a frame, marking the location of the four butt hinges. The two outside hinges are 2" in from the ends. The inside hinges are 19½" in from the ends. Recess the hinges. Use 3/4" X 6" lumber for the frame and two braces. The braces are attached to the under-side of the drop bench with the hinges reversed. Hooks and eyes hold the drop bench closed. Add a peg-board back for hanging tools.

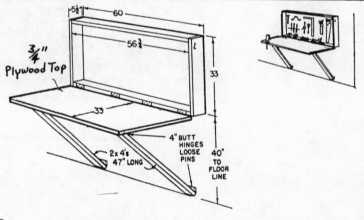

5½
60
56¾

¾" Plywood Top

33

33

4" BUTT HINGES LOOSE PINS

2 x 4's 47" LONG

40" TO FLOOR LINE

## SAWBOX

CENTER LINE

Top
3/4" X 5" X 25"

Support
3/4" X 6½" X 25"

Box
8" X 16" X 21"

Legs
3/4" X 3 5/8" X 31"

1"

Just build a box or use an old drawer. Add four legs and you have a sturdy sawbox. Find the center of box then clamp leg 1" from bottom corner of box. Mark and cut off the part extending up from center line. Repeat for other legs. Clamp legs in place with an on-edge board between them. Screw in place.

## FLUSH-CUTTING HACKSAW

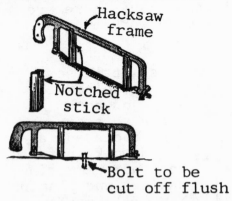

Hacksaw frame

Notched stick

Bolt to be cut off flush

If you have to cut off a screw or bolt flush with a flat surface, this little trick will save you lots of time. Turn hacksaw blade sideways. Put two small notched sticks about 3½" long between blade and frame to hold blade out. Tighten blade and you are ready to cut away.

## MINI GREASE-GUN

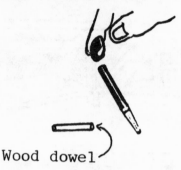

Wood dowel

You can make a great mini grease-gun from the bottom section of an old mechanical pencil. Remove the mechanism, fill the lower barrel with grease, and use a snug-fitting wood dowel for a plunger. It's excellent for lubricating small, hard-to-reach parts.

DO-IT-YOURSELFER'S LAW
If it can break, spring a leak, or get lost, it will invariably do so on a Sunday or holiday when the stores are closed.

## POOR MAN'S LOCK NUT

Spur corner

The next time you need to lock a nut onto a bolt but don't have a lockwasher, just flatten one end of the nut with a hammer. This little spur will cause the nut to tip slightly, making it grip the bolt threads tightly.

## OVERCOMING A SLOPPY VISE

Hooks hold spring
Screen-door spring around stationary jaw

After long use an old vise often becomes worn. Threads become loose making the jaws insensitive to small movements. You can overcome this lag by stretching a screen-door spring around the stationary jaw and hooking the ends to the rear corners.

## U-BUILD SHAFT BEARINGS

Handy bench stand for saws, grinding wheels, or sanding disks can easily be made from old pipe fittings.

Utilizing old galvanized iron or steel pipe fittings allows you to build everything from heavy-duty bench tool stands to excellent heavy-duty shaft bearings for power tools--all at very low cost. Most of the materials required, such as "T" pipe fittings, floor flanges, and short, threaded pipe nipples, should all be available at your local junk yard or salvage yard. (Look in the yellow pages of your phone book under "Wreckers" or "Salvage.") Even bronze bushings and old ball bearings (from an auto generator) can be found there. Of course, all of these things can be bought new at most hardware or plumbing supply stores, but that sort of takes the fun out of it. Plus, it will cost you more. The only tools needed to build your own shaft bearings are an electric drill and a small high-speed grinder for reaming or grinding out the threads in the pipe "T" for bearings. For some special applications you might need some parts welded. NOTE: All bronze bushing shaft bearings should have an oil cup installed as shown for proper lubrication. You can make your own oil cup by press fitting ¼" copper tubing into a pre-drilled hole in the pipe "T." Be sure to drill through both the pipe "T" and bronze bushing as shown.

1" Pipe "T"

Threads reamed out on both ends for bearings

1" Pipe nipple about 4"-6" long threaded at both ends

Floor Flange is bolted to workbench top.

Auto generator Bearing press fitted into "T"

V-Pulley 2" dia.

½" Steel shaft threaded for attaching grinding wheel, saw, etc.

Oil Cup

Steel Shaft

Bronze Bushing Press fitted

Pipe Nipple

Shaft bearing from pipe fitting

Oil cup

"T"

Long nipple

Floor flange

Threads reamed or bored out for bushing

Adjustable Base

Weld

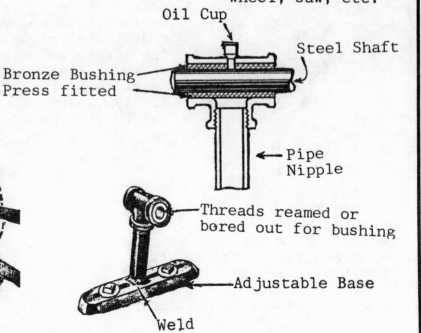

## MINI ARBOR-PRESS

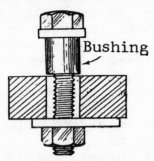
Bushing

Using a capscrew, washer, nut, and a drilled steel plate, you can make a mini arbor-press. Perfect for seating small bushings or bearings.

## SIMPLE THRUST BEARING

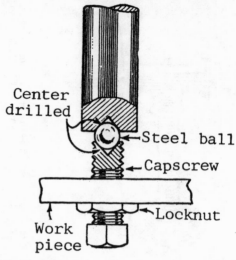
Center drilled
Steel ball
Capscrew
Locknut
Work piece

This simple-to-build thrust bearing will take both end and side thrust. Designed to be used only in low-speed operations. It can be adjusted to take up end play, and is easily assembled.

## TIGHTEN UP WORN MOTOR BEARINGS

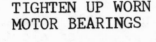
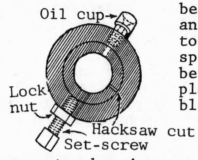
Oil cup
Lock nut
Hacksaw cut
Set-screw

Don't be hoggish. Pass this book around.

Worn motor bearings on small electric motors can be tightened for further service. Remove bearings and with a hacksaw slit them along one side. Take care to remove burrs. Drill and tap each bearing on the underside for ¼" set-screw. Replace bearings with slitted side at right angles to the set-screw. Tighten set-screw against bearing until motor shaft runs snugly, but freely. Bearings can now be easily readjusted for wear.

**You Can Save a Bundle**
by doing-it-yourself

## SIMPLE METHOD OF REMOVING STUDS

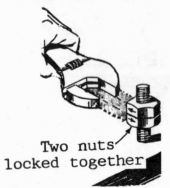
Two nuts locked together

You can remove threaded studs when the threaded portion is accessible by turning two nuts together tightly on the stud. Fit your wrench onto the lower nut and turn off nuts and stud together. Sometimes heating a tight stud will loosen it.

WORKING MAN'S LAW
There will always be, another unpaid bill. Usually overdue!

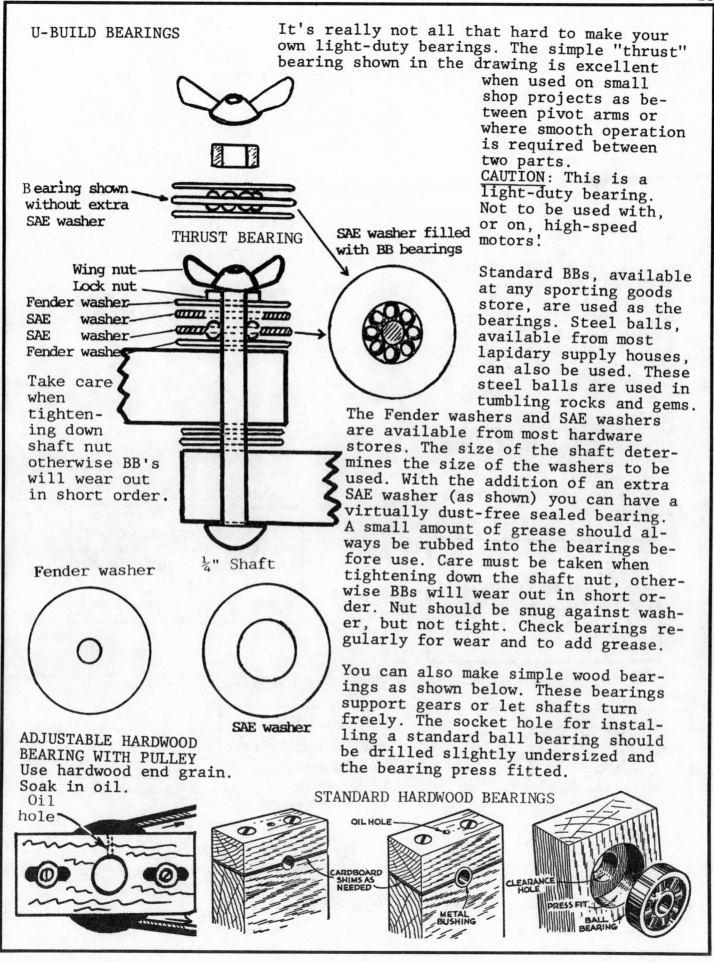

## U-BUILD BEARINGS

It's really not all that hard to make your own light-duty bearings. The simple "thrust" bearing shown in the drawing is excellent when used on small shop projects as between pivot arms or where smooth operation is required between two parts.

CAUTION: This is a light-duty bearing. Not to be used with, or on, high-speed motors!

Bearing shown without extra SAE washer

THRUST BEARING

SAE washer filled with BB bearings

Wing nut
Lock nut
Fender washer
SAE washer
SAE washer
Fender washer

Take care when tightening down shaft nut otherwise BB's will wear out in short order.

¼" Shaft

Standard BBs, available at any sporting goods store, are used as the bearings. Steel balls, available from most lapidary supply houses, can also be used. These steel balls are used in tumbling rocks and gems. The Fender washers and SAE washers are available from most hardware stores. The size of the shaft determines the size of the washers to be used. With the addition of an extra SAE washer (as shown) you can have a virtually dust-free sealed bearing. A small amount of grease should always be rubbed into the bearings before use. Care must be taken when tightening down the shaft nut, otherwise BBs will wear out in short order. Nut should be snug against washer, but not tight. Check bearings regularly for wear and to add grease.

You can also make simple wood bearings as shown below. These bearings support gears or let shafts turn freely. The socket hole for installing a standard ball bearing should be drilled slightly undersized and the bearing press fitted.

Fender washer

SAE washer

ADJUSTABLE HARDWOOD BEARING WITH PULLEY
Use hardwood end grain. Soak in oil.
Oil hole

STANDARD HARDWOOD BEARINGS

OIL HOLE

CARDBOARD SHIMS AS NEEDED

METAL BUSHING

CLEARANCE HOLE

PRESS FIT

BALL BEARING

## CONVERT FLAT PULLEY TO V-BELT DRIVE

Stove bolts

V-Belt

Flat Belt Pulley

By using two old lengths of V-belt you can convert a large flat pulley to V-belt drive. The two lengths of old V-belt are reversed and bolted to the pulley, so that the wide side of the belts are against the face of the pulley. The space between the belts should be just wide enough for the drive. This method should not be used for small flat pulleys due to the difficulty in reversing belts on a small radius.

**Do-It-Yourselfers Have More Fun!**

## SPLICING A V-Belt

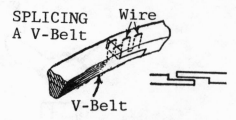

Wire

V-Belt

In an emergency you can usually splice a broken V-belt. With a sharp knife or hacksaw, cut a half-lap into the belt at the break. Half-lap the ends together and, with an awl, punch eight holes through the belt at the points shown. Lace the ends together with steel wire. The belt will be just slightly shorter than before the break.

REPAIRMAN'S LAW

After being asked to fix a broken appliance at least forty times, You finally get around to it, only to find your wife fixed it with a hairpin.

## THE IRS!

Blaugh!

Clip and mail along with your next Income Tax return—Then send for our low Rent-a-barrel rates!

## O.K. FOLKS ALL TOGETHER NOW

Lets send a big kiss to our favorite Washington charity

Reprinted from the Poor Man's Catalog #4.
PLEASE send all contributions to the "bail out" the Poor Man's Fund, in care of the Federal Penitentiary!

## U-BUILD PULLEYS

Most craftpersons who build their own power tools, light machinery, or even toys, will sooner or later find that they need drive pulleys. These simple little devices transfer power thru the use of belts. You can buy commercially made pulleys in many sizes and price ranges, but you will save both time and bucks by building your own. The home-built pulley can be just as strong, and last just as long as the store-bought ones. Better yet, you can build them to order by using scraps from your shop. Drive belts can be anything from nylon rope to a flat leather belt. We have even used electrical tape and strips cut from an old rubber inner tube as drive belts on small projects.

Small drive pulleys can be made from hardwood dowels. Force fit onto motor shaft then file a groove after turning motor on.

With power tools or machinery, you should stay with the standard V-belt to insure a complete transfer of power. The only tools really needed to build pulleys are a circle cutter and electric drill. (The drill preferably in a drill stand.) Several files and a pair of metal shears would help if you are going to reinforce your pulley with metal side plates. Metal side reinforcing plates are simply metal disks usually 1/32" to 1/16" in thickness made from sheet aluminum, brass, or steel. The actual pulley should be made only from hardwood, or hard, tempered composition board. Plywood can be used if the sides are reinforced with metal disks. Very small pulleys can be glued together. Pulleys 2" or larger should be bolted or riveted together.

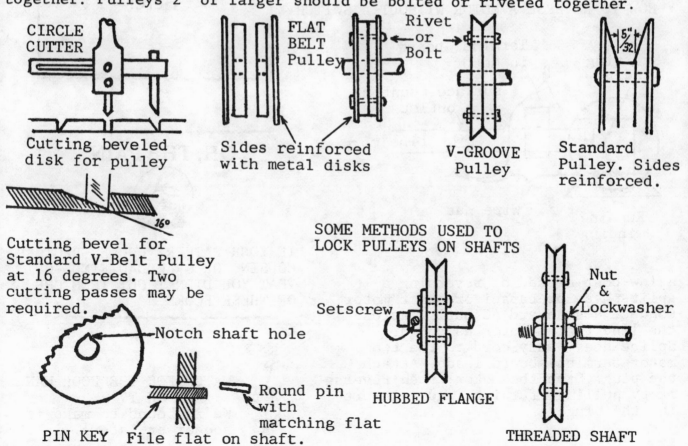

**CIRCLE CUTTER**

Cutting beveled disk for pulley

Cutting bevel for Standard V-Belt Pulley at 16 degrees. Two cutting passes may be required.

**FLAT BELT Pulley**

Sides reinforced with metal disks

Rivet or Bolt

**V-GROOVE Pulley**

5"/32

Standard Pulley. Sides reinforced.

SOME METHODS USED TO LOCK PULLEYS ON SHAFTS

Notch shaft hole

Round pin with matching flat

**PIN KEY** File flat on shaft.

Setscrew

**HUBBED FLANGE**

Nut & Lockwasher

**THREADED SHAFT**

## REMOVE TIGHT PULLEYS WITH C-CLAMPS

Pulley

NUT

BOLT

C-Clamp

Hardwood block

If you don't have a gear puller, you can usually remove tight-fitting motor pulleys with two C-clamps. Fit a hardwood block with a bolt and nut as shown. Clamps are hooked over the pulley and the hardwood block centered on the shaft so that tightening the clamps applies pressure behind pulley.

## EMERGENCY BRUSH REPAIR

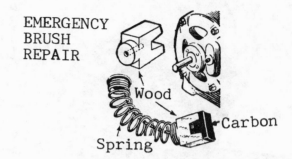

Wood

Carbon

Spring

If the brush in an electric motor wears down or breaks, and you have no replacement, just shape a small piece of wood to slip into the brush holder. Slot one end and round the other to accept the brush spring. Then shape the commutator end of the brush to slip into the slot in the wood. This will lengthen the brush, allowing it to be used until it can be replaced.

## HOW TO REVERSE A MOTOR WITHOUT A SWITCH

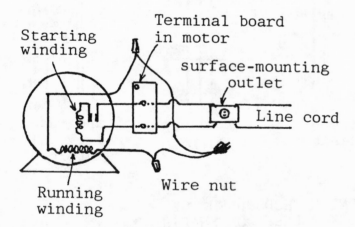

Starting winding

Terminal board in motor

surface-mounting outlet

Line cord

Running winding

Wire nut

A low-cost method of reversing a split-phase or capacitor-start motor. Connect a standard AC outlet across the line to the motor as shown. Splice heavy-duty cord to the two motor-terminal board leads. Attach the plug. Stop the motor; then reverse it by pulling, turning, and reinserting the plug.

Doodle Here!

## OH, THE PAIN

IF YOUR FATHER, UNCLE, BROTHER, COUSIN, OR GRANDDAD FINDS OUT THAT YOU DIDN'T GET THEM ONE OF THESE BOOKS!

WATCH FOR THE POOR MAN ON TV
We're bound to make it sooner or later!

# DETERMINING POWER TOOL SPEEDS AND PULLEY SIZES

Most craftsmen sooner or later, will run into the problem of determining the correct speeds needed for various power tools. And what size pulleys are needed to achive these speeds. In most machine-tool operations the speed of the tool is most important. The only exception being those tools operated by direct drive such as the grinder shown.

**DIRECT DRIVE**
*(Grinder)*

Most home workshop power tools are powered by fractional horsepower motors. The most usual being the 1750 RPM electric motor. Sometimes, a higher RPM motor, such as a 3500 RPM motor must be stepped down in speed to make it useable on the tool. This is usually done through the use of belts and pulleys. The speed of the tool can be varied in spite of the fact that the speed of the motor remains constant. The craftsman who is faced with the problem of setting up a tool to operate at a specific speed should find the formulas listed here most useful.

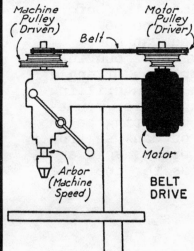

*Machine Pulley (Driven)* — *Belt* — *Motor Pulley (Driver)* — *Motor* — *Arbor (Machine Speed)* — **BELT DRIVE**

Formula 1. is used to determine speed of the tool when diameters of motor pulley, tool pulley, and speed of the motor is known.

No. 1 $\text{R.P.M. of machine} = \dfrac{\text{Dia. of motor pulley} \times \text{R.P.M. of motor}}{\text{Dia. of machine pulley}}$

Formula 2. is used to determine size of the tool pulley needed for a specific speed when motor RPM, size of motor pulley, and required speed are known.

No. 2 $\text{Dia. of machine pulley} = \dfrac{\text{Dia. of motor pulley} \times \text{R.P.M. of motor}}{\text{R.P.M. of machine}}$

Formula 3. is used to determine the RPM speed of the motor required to drive the tool at a specified speed when size of motor and tool pulleys are known.

No. 3 $\text{R.P.M. of motor} = \dfrac{\text{Dia. of machine pulley} \times \text{R.P.M. of machine}}{\text{Dia. of motor pulley}}$

**MACHINE** — *Machine Pulley (Driven)* — **JACKSHAFT** — *Jackshaft Driver Pulley* — *Belt* — **MOTOR** — *Motor Pulley (Driver)* — *Belt* — *Jackshaft Driven Pulley* — *Motor* — *Arbor (Machine speed)* — **JACKSHAFT DRIVE**

Formula 4. is used to determine the size of the motor pulley required to drive a tool at a specified speed when the speed of the motor and size of the tool pulley are known

No. 4 $\text{Dia. of motor pulley} = \dfrac{\text{Dia. of machine pulley} \times \text{R.P.M. of machine}}{\text{R.P.M. of motor}}$

Formulas 5. to 8. inclusive, are used when a jackshaft is introduced into the power pulley train. A jackshaft can make a tool operate at extremely low, or extremely high speeds, as well as almost any intermediate speed.

Formula 5. Will give the speed of the tool when all other factors are known.

No. 5 $\text{R.P.M. of machine} = \dfrac{\text{Dia. of motor pulley (X) R.P.M. of motor (X) dia. of jackshaft-driver pulley}}{\text{Dia. of jackshaft-driven pulley (X) dia. of machine pulley}}$

Formula 6. is used to determine motor pulley size when all info. is known.

No. 6 $\text{Dia. of motor pulley} = \dfrac{\text{Dia. of jackshaft-driven pulley (X) dia. of machine pulley (X) R.P.M. of machine}}{\text{R.P.M. of motor (X) dia. of jackshaft-driver pulley}}$

Formula 7. is used to determine jackshaft-driven pulley size.

No. 7 $\text{Dia. of jackshaft-driven pulley} = \dfrac{\text{Dia. of motor pulley (X) R.P.M. of motor (X) dia. of jackshaft-driver pulley}}{\text{Dia. of machine pulley (X) R.P.M. of machine}}$

Formula 8. is used to determine jackshaft-driver pulley size.

No. 8 $\text{Dia. of jackshaft-driver pulley} = \dfrac{\text{Dia. of jackshaft-driven pulley (X) dia. of machine pulley (X) R.P.M. (mach)}}{\text{Dia. of motor pulley (X) R.P.M. of motor}}$

**Think
do it yourself!**

## UNIVERSAL MOTOR MOUNT USING ANGLE-BRACKET LEGS

Cut from angle iron

Salvaged electric motors from old appliances usually need a motor mounting before they can be used to power shop tools. You can make your own universal mounting by cutting sections of angle iron as shown, then drilling holes at each end for mounting motor, and bolting to tool bench. You can use iron angle corner braces sold at hardware stores for the same purpose.

## DUAL MOTOR POWER

Running in tandem

Alternate method

Drive pulley on longer shaft

Clamps

Garden hose

The doubling up of two light motors can give you the power of one big motor. Two ¼-hp motors deliver ½-hp so long as both ¼-hp motors have the same speed rating. Two methods of doing this are shown above. The top two motors running in tandem must run on the same size pulleys.

WHERE OH WHERE OLD
TOOL KIT OF MINE,
HAVE THE KIDS LEFT YOU,
THIS TIME?

## IMPROVISED MOTOR MOUNT

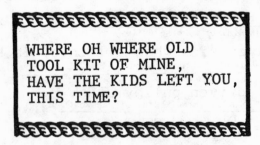

Another method of mounting a salvaged electric motor is to build a "motor cradle" from scrap 2" stock. Use a 2" X 6" for the base, and cradle the motor with two pieces of 2" X 2" stock. Use a 3" strip of sheet metal as the hold-down strap. Countersink the heads of the hold-down bolts.

## TWO SLIDING MOTOR MOUNTS

One way for the craftsperson to cut down costs
is to utilize power tools to their fullest advantage, at the lowest possible cost. One way
of doing this is to use just one electric motor
to power all your belt-driven tools. Our "Rail
Mount" plan shows how you can set up an entire
workshop using just one motor mounted on rails.
By sliding the motor forward or backward on angle
iron rails, you can service all of your belt-driven
tools. Our "Rod Mount" plan shows a simple method
of mounting a permanent motor that allows fine
adjustment of belt tension.

### RAIL MOUNT

Designed to service any number of belt-driven tools,
the Rail Mount is adjustable laterally for fast belt
tensioning. The lower block of the mount is slotted to
slide freely on 1" X 1" angle iron rails spaced about
5" apart. The center piece of the upper assembly to which the motor is
bolted slides on two grooved members screwed to the lower block. This is
made adjustable crosswise by means of a bolt passing through a flat iron
brace into a nut embedded into the wood. Power tools which can be operated either clockwise or counter-clockwise, such as a jigsaw, disk sander, etc., should be mounted along the rear side of the workbench so that other tools that must run clockwise can be driven without twisting the drive belt.

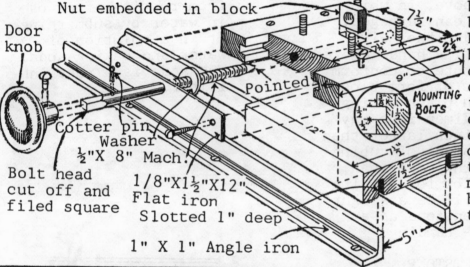

Nut embedded in block
Door knob
Cotter pin
Washer
½"X 8" Mach.
Bolt head cut off and filed square
1/8"X1½"X12" Flat iron Slotted 1" deep
1" X 1" Angle iron
Pointed
MOUNTING BOLTS
7½" 2¼" 9" 7½" 5"

### ROD MOUNT

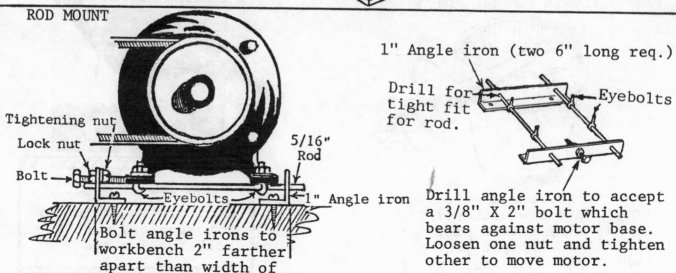

Tightening nut
Lock nut
Bolt
Eyebolts
5/16" Rod
1" Angle iron
Bolt angle irons to workbench 2" farther apart than width of motor base.

1" Angle iron (two 6" long req.)
Drill for tight fit for rod.
Eyebolts
Drill angle iron to accept a 3/8" X 2" bolt which bears against motor base. Loosen one nut and tighten other to move motor.

## TUBE BENDING JIG

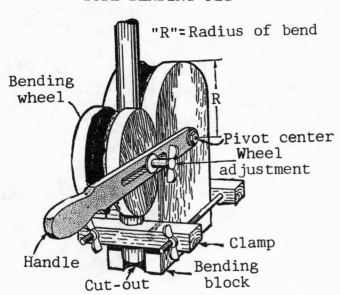

"R"= Radius of bend

Bending wheel

R

Pivot center
Wheel adjustment

Handle

Cut-out

Clamp

Bending block

This little tool which can be made from scraps, consists of a wooden form block with a groove, in which the extent of a bend can be gaged. Grooves can be formed either with machine or hand tools. A hand-levered wooden wheel forces tube to conform with contoured groove of form block. A clamp holds tube in place during bending. All groove dimensions may be a fraction of an inch larger than contours of biggest piece of tubing to be bent. Bend tubing more than required angle to allow for "spring back." NOTE: There will be a slight change in tubing dimensions as a natural result of the bending.

## FLOWER POT WHETSTONE

Need to sharpen a knife but don't have a whetstone? Try an old clay flower pot. Using the rim of the pot you can hone a knife to razor sharpness.

## RUST INHIBITOR

You can save steel wool from rusting after use in water by submerging it in a solution of water and baking soda. The soda is a rust inhibitor.

© 1980 VOLK

## SIMPLE SPEED REDUCER

Build this little jackshaft stand and you can reduce the rpm speed of any power tool that uses a separate motor for power. Perfect for lowering speeds for metal cutting, sawing, sanding, and even wood or metal turning on a lathe. The jackshaft, built as shown in the drawing, will give you a 10:1 speed reduction. You can, of course, change the speed reduction ratios by changing the sizes of the pulleys used. The jackshaft stand and mounting board are both made from 3/4" plywood. If you can mount pulleys on both sides of your motor shaft, it will make it much easier to shift speeds fast. Otherwise, you must turn your motor around when shifting back to normal speed. Mount ball bearings in the two sides of the jackshaft stand to accept the pulley shaft. Note the use of a piano hinge along the bottom of the stand that allows it to tilt forward, keeping both pulley drive belts taut when in use.

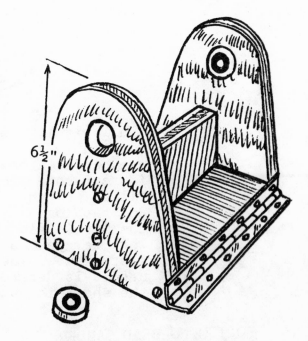

The heart of the Speed Reducer is this little jackshaft stand made of 3/4" plywood. The width is the same as the motor used for power.

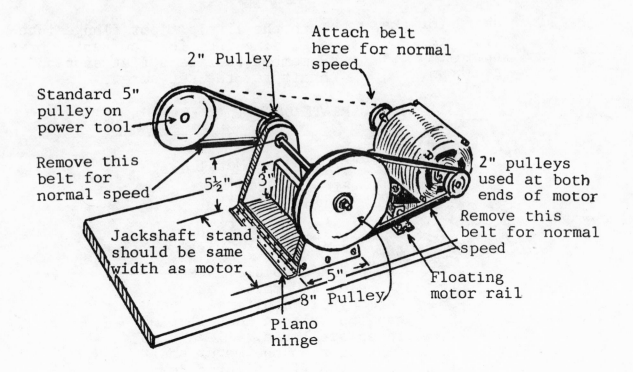

Attach belt here for normal speed

2" Pulley

Standard 5" pulley on power tool

Remove this belt for normal speed

5½"

3"

Jackshaft stand should be same width as motor

2" pulleys used at both ends of motor

Remove this belt for normal speed

Floating motor rail

5"

8" Pulley

Piano hinge

# A USEFUL ITEM

## Pipe Floor Flange

The lowly little pipe floor flange
(available at most hardware stores)
can become a most useful accessory
in your home shop. By reaming or
filing out the threads, and drilling
and tapping a ¼" hole for a set-screw,
the little floor flange can do some real
work for you as shown in the three projects below. The size of the flange
needed is determined by the diameter of
the shaft it is to be used with.

## POLISHING HEAD SANDER

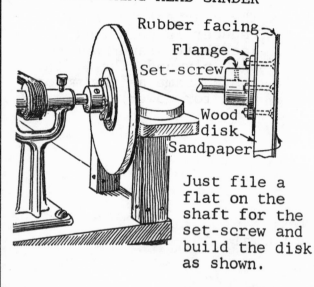

Just file a
flat on the
shaft for the
set-screw and
build the disk
as shown.

## DRILL PRESS SANDING DRUM

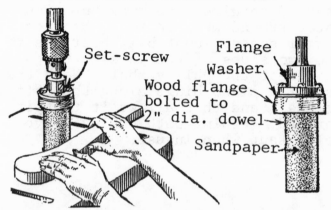

Turn the little floor flange into
a sanding drum for your drill press.
Remember to file a flat spot on the
shaft for the set-screw.

## MINI FACEPLATE LATHE

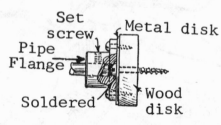

Using an old 1725 RPM
electric motor found
in many old appliances, you
can improvise a neat little
faceplate lathe. File a
flat spot on the motor shaft
where you will tighten down
the set-screw.

## POOR MAN'S ECCENTRIC

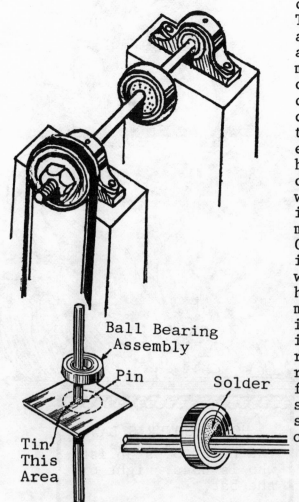

Ball Bearing Assembly

Pin

Tin This Area

Solder

You really don't need a machine shop to build your own eccentric or cam. You can do the job in your home workshop. To build an excellent rolling eccentric, all you need is a ball-bearing assembly, a drill rod for a shaft, and scrap sheet metal. Locate a bearing with an inside diameter large enough to allow your eccentric the required throw. The shaft center must offset from the center of the bearing by half the amount of linear motion required. Drill a press fit hole for pin about half way through the drill rod shaft. Tin this pin and shaft where it will contact the bearing solder insert. Slide a scrap piece of sheet metal up the shaft about 1/8" from pin. Clamp shaft upright, and position bearing for required throw. Wrap bearing in wet rag to keep from over heating. Apply heat to shaft about 1" above bearing and melt bar solder against shaft, allowing it to flow down and fill inside of bearing. BELOW: Build cam from bar of cold rolled steel. Grind and shape lobe to required throw. Drill two holes offset for throw. Pin shaft and fill with bar solder as instructed above. NOTE: Pin should protrude about half the amount of eccentricity.

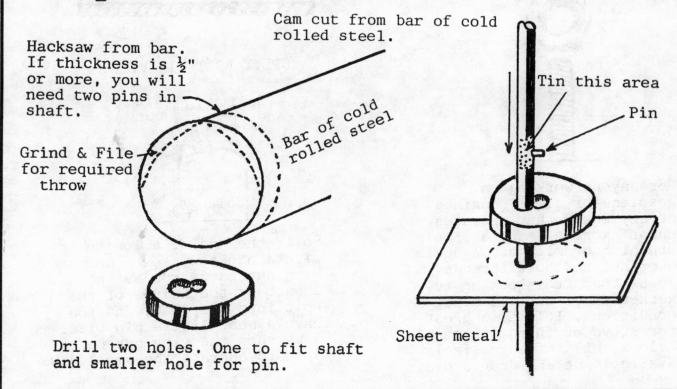

Cam cut from bar of cold rolled steel.

Hacksaw from bar. If thickness is ½" or more, you will need two pins in shaft.

Bar of cold rolled steel

Grind & File for required throw

Tin this area

Pin

Sheet metal

Drill two holes. One to fit shaft and smaller hole for pin.

## POOR MAN'S KEYHOLE SAW

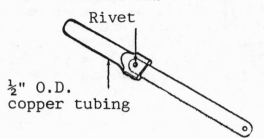

Rivet

½" O.D.
copper tubing

Using a 6" piece of ½"
O.D. copper tubing for
a handle and a broken
hacksaw blade, you have
a most useful little saw.
Just partly flatten one
end of the tubing and
insert the stub of the
hacksaw blade, flatten
tubing further, drill
and rivet.

©VOLK

## HONEYMOONER'S LAW
You have to establish
who is boss, right off
the bat.

## HIGH HEAT NO-LOCK FOR NUTS & BOLTS

For anyone working on
gasoline or diesel engines
or any motor that operates
under extreme heat, a simple
brushing of milk of magnesia
over nut and bolt threads
keeps them from locking together under extreme heat
conditions. It's also great
for stove or furnace install-
ations. Milk of magnesia is
available at any drug store.

## SPLIT BOLT PIN VISE

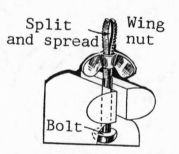

Split
and spread   Wing nut

Bolt

Split the end of a long bolt
with a hacksaw, screw down a
wing nut backwards as shown,
then bend the halves of the
bolt into a spread, and you
have a neat little pin vise.
Just turn the wing nut up or
down to operate the small jaws.

## DRILL STAND

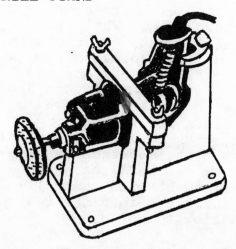

Your portable electric drill can do a lot more than just drill holes. Build this simple drill stand and convert your electric drill into a stationary power tool. Built as shown, you can use it for sharpening knives and tools, grinding down small parts, wire brush cleaning, disk sanding, and buffing and polishing. The stand is built from scrap wood and you determine the exact dimensions directly from your own electric drill. Just lay out a cardboard pattern by tracing around your drill. Cut out the pattern and use it to transfer your drill's image directly to 3/4" stock, then jigsaw to shape. Follow the same procedure for the "U"-shaped part (dimensions are determined by the size of your drill). Notch and fit parts together and mount on base. Install drill into stand and check carefully to insure that drill chuck is straight and level. Check with a level before final assembly. If necessary, plane off any high spots along bottom of stand until the chuck is perfectly level. Assemble and finish as you prefer.

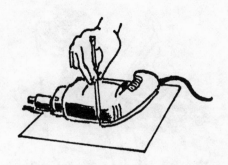

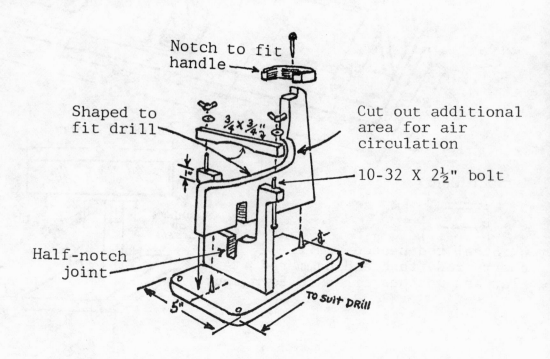

Notch to fit handle

Shaped to fit drill

¾ X ¾"

Cut out additional area for air circulation

10-32 X 2½" bolt

Half-notch joint

5"

TO SUIT DRILL

## DRILL-DRIVEN LATHE

Once you have built the drill stand for your portable electric drill, you can use it to power the light-duty lathe shown below. While it is light-duty, you may be surprised at the jobs that it can do--from turning tool handles and fancy wooden parts, to actually shaping soft metals with hand tools. The lathe will handle wood stock up to 18" long and 3" in thickness, depending upon the power of your electric drill. Use 3/4" stock for the bed of the lathe. Mount the lathe bed on 1" X 1" X 8" wood blocks at each end. Cut out the ¼" adjustment slots for the sliding tailstock and tool rest. Mount the drill stand, with the electric drill, to the lathe bed using bolts and wing nuts. The most important measurement is between the drill chuck and the tailstock of the lathe. The tailstock ¼" threaded rod must be in perfect alignment with the drill chuck. NOTE: The tailstock threaded rod has a notch cut into the rear for screwdriver adjustment. Follow directions below to build.

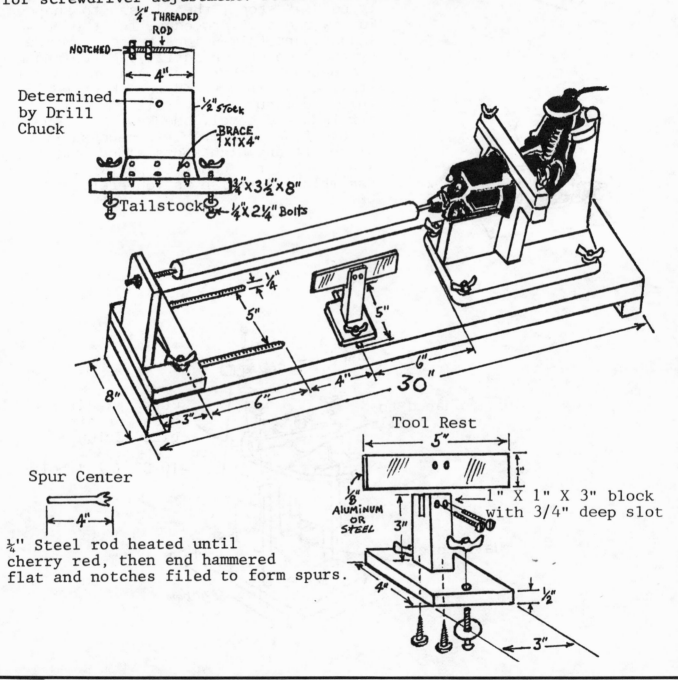

¼" THREADED ROD

NOTCHED

Determined by Drill Chuck

½" STOCK

BRACE 1 X 1 X 4"

¾" X 3½" X 8"

Tailstock

¼ X 2¼" Bolts

Spur Center

¼" Steel rod heated until cherry red, then end hammered flat and notches filed to form spurs.

Tool Rest

1" X 1" X 3" block with 3/4" deep slot

⅛ ALUMINUM OR STEEL

## POOR MAN'S SPRING WINDER

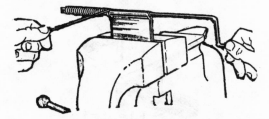

Compression    Tension

I must have a thousand springs of assorted sizes. But when I need one, they are all the wrong size. Using a rod as a mandrel, bend a crank on one end of a rod with a slightly smaller diameter than the inside diameter of the spring you wish to produce. Saw a slot across the far end of the crank rod to engage spring wire. Fold a scrap piece of sheet metal to form a crank bearing and insert into vise as shown. Start spring with slotted end of crank rod at the edge of the bearing. Insert spring wire into slot and start cranking. Control pitch of spring by varying the rate at which you push crank rod through bearing as you turn crank.

## POOR MAN'S "DIE"

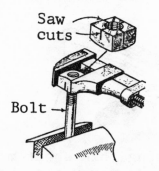

Saw cuts

Bolt

When you need to clean bolt threads of clogging rust or paint, or if the threads are damaged, just hacksaw slots into the correct size nut as shown. Spread the cuts slightly and start this side of the nut down on the bolt threads. Cleans them right up.

### FATHER'S LAW

Two can live as cheaply as one, only if they live with you!

## BOLT THREAD LUBRICANT
Carpenter's pencil

The lead in a carpenter's pencil applied to bolt threads will cover them with a lubricating coating of graphite making them much easier to remove later. Rub the lead in thoroughly.

## SHEET METAL SANDWICH

When cutting thin sheet metal
with a hacksaw you can get a
truer cut with less bending
by sandwiching the sheet metal
between two pieces of scrap
wood and sawing through all
three pieces.

## INSULATED STAPLES

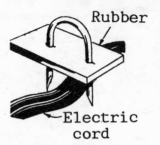

When running electrical
wiring, you should always
use insulated staples. Of
course, this will be the
time that you don't have
any. Cut small squares from
an old inner tube and you
are in business.

WHAT FLY?

## POOR MAN'S MINI CHUCK

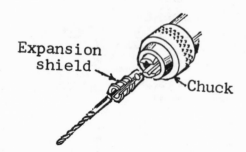

Once in a while you will run
into the problem of tiny drill
bits that are too small for the
chuck of your electric drill or
drill press. Insert the small
drill into an expansion shield
and insert the expansion shield
into the chuck.

## TWO WAYS OF STRAIGHTENING
## WIRE

A discarded table fork
makes a convenient tool
for removing kinks and
bends from wire. Wire
is passed in and out
through the tines, then
pulled to draw and stra-
ighten it. Another method
is to roll over the wire
on a flat surface with a
cold iron.

## LATHE DRUM AND DISK SANDERS

Just as your portable electric drill can do a lot more than drill holes, your u-build lathe can do more than just turn wood. Remove the tool rest from the lathe, build the simple little rig shown below, and you have a drum sander. Take a tin can, cut out both ends, taper two wooden caps to a snug fit inside the tin can. Center drill a ¼" hole in each cap, add a ¼" X 12" threaded rod with nuts at each end, and glue a sheet of sand-paper around the can to form your drum sander.

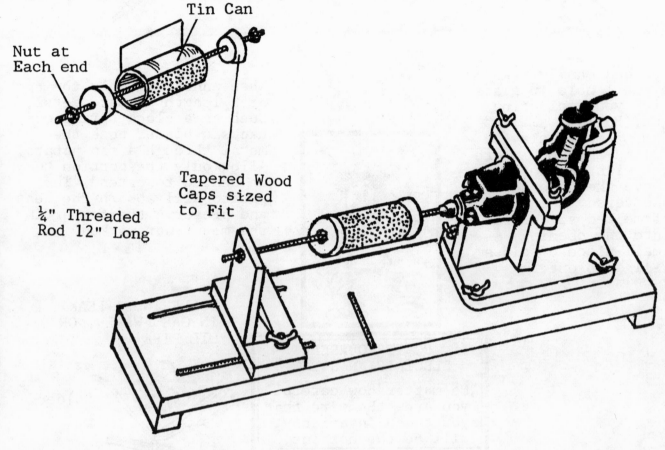

Tin Can

Nut at
Each end

Tapered Wood
Caps sized
to Fit

¼" Threaded
Rod 12" Long

Add a disk sanding unit to your electric drill. Build a small wooden table to fit across the lathe bed, and you have a lathe disk sander.

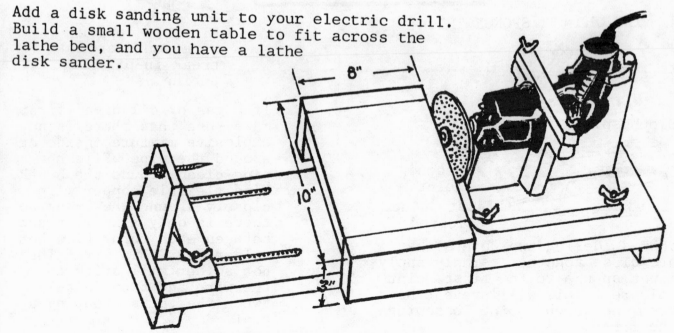

8"

10"

3"

## DRILL GLASS WITH YOUR SOLDERING GUN

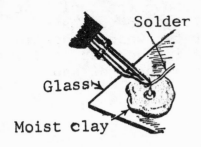

You can easily make a small hole in glass with your soldering gun. Build a small dam of moist clay around the spot where you wish the hole. Leave the hole spot uncovered. Let a drop of melted solder fall into the opening. A small piece of glass will drop out.

## RAW POTATO HEAT DAM

When annealing only the end of a length of hard metal, such as a clock spring or hacksaw blade, push the metal through a raw potato. Allow only the portion to be heated to extend. The potato will absorb the heat and preserve the temper in the metal not worked.

## DO-IT-YOURSELF ELECTRICIAN'S LAW

No matter how careful you are, the wire that you touch invariably will be the hot one.

## SOLDERING A LEAK IN GAS, WATER, OR OIL PIPE

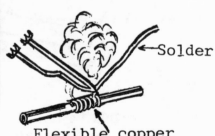

Solder

Flexible copper wire wound around break in pipe or tubing.

If a gas or oil pipe, first make sure that there is no explosive mixture inside or around the pipe. File the pipe clean around the break. Wind flexible copper wire closely around the break so there is only a small space between each turn. Flow hot solder over this wire. The hot solder will stick to the wire and flow in between the turns creating a seal.

## THE OLD WET SPONGE TRICK

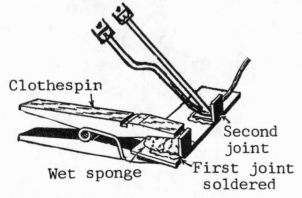

Clothespin

Second joint

First joint soldered

Wet sponge

When soldering two joints that are close together, simply apply a wet sponge to the first joint soldered. This will prevent heat from the second joint loosening the first.

# SOLDERING GUN TIPS

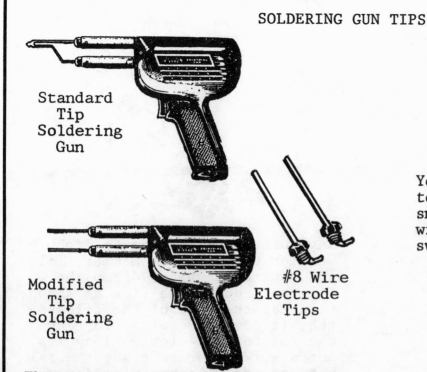

Standard
Tip
Soldering
Gun

Modified
Tip
Soldering
Gun

#8 Wire
Electrode
Tips

Your soldering gun is a made-to-order demagnetizer for small tools. Just insert and withdraw the tool with the switch on.

Hacksaw a slot down the middle of the blade.

There are a number of things that you can do to increase the usefulness of your soldering gun. Sometimes it's almost impossible to solder a clean, tight joint in a very tight spot. It's also hard to try and solder tempered metals to heavier metals without drawing the temper. Using the home-made tip shown above, you can do both. The two short 3" sections of #8 wire act as electrodes in your soldering gun. They will give low-voltage, high-amperage current through the metals you are soldering. The current flowing through the work heats it similarly to a wire in an electric heater. All the heat is concentrated between the two wire electrodes. The work itself becomes part of your soldering gun circuit. For best results, use a heavy-duty gun of 250 to 275 watts. Tin each tip by laying a strip of flux-core solder across the tips and applying heat. To use, simply bend the ends of the wires before each job so that they straddle the work. You want the shortest possible path between the wire electrodes, then hold firmly against the work.

Silver-solder an old table-knife blade to your soldering gun's replaceable tip and you can slice through polystyrene like a hot knife through butter. Hacksaw a slot down the middle of the blade for better heat distribution.

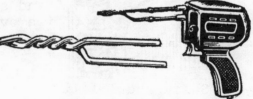

Make your own long-life, heavy-duty soldering tip by twisting and bending 12-gauge copper wire as shown. Lasts much longer than single wire tips.

34

POOR MAN'S SHEET-METAL BRAKE

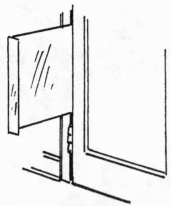

FILE    KNURLING

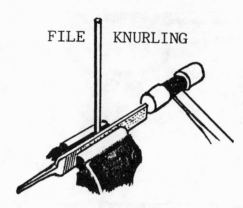

The next time you need to
bend light sheet metal but
don't have a sheet-metal
brake, try using a door jamb.
Makes perfect right-angle bends.

Any soft metal rod can be lightly
knurled using just a hammer, file,
and your bench vise. Clamp the
file and rod in the vise as shown,
then tap the edge of the file so
that it moves edgewise, forcing
the rod to roll slowly along its
surface. Wood or soft sheet metal
between the file and vise jaw
will protect the file.

# BORROW YOUR OWN MONEY BACK!

ANY AMOUNT

AT BELOW THE PRIME RATE*

LITTLE COLLATERAL NEEDED

(* interest compounded daily)
Just to show you that our hearts are
in the right place, the friendly
folks of the OPEC Finance Company
are going to make things easy for
you. Now, for the first time, you
can borrow your own money back at
low, low, interest rates. Whatever your needs, we have it. In fact,
we have it all! Just mail your
home mortgage, along with your wife,
and state the amount required. Will
we ever take care of you! Mail to:

OPEC FINANCE COMPANY
Gushing Oil Street
Middle East, Zip-IOU

Sheik Abdul I'll
    Stickittou
Chairman of the Board

They already
took care of
me!

Another great service brought to you by OPEC
Organization of Petroleum Extorting Countries

# Energy

The energy saving projects shown below are not available in <u>this</u> catalog. They are available in our self-published Poor Man's Catalog #5.

My wife wanted one of those little gas-saving economy cars, so....

## POOR MAN'S DUAL FUELS

By now, most everyone is aware that alcohol mixed with gasoline (gasohol) can power the family buggy. Pure alcohol (ethanol) can be used to fuel your car if you modify the carburetor. Plus, the use of pure alcohol as a motor fuel has some excellent side benefits. It burns cleanly, and actually acts as a cleaning agent inside your car's engine--no catalytic converter or anti-pollution junk required. More important, alcohol is not as dangerously volatile as gasoline. How many lives and horribly burned people could have been saved by using alcohol as a motor fuel? And strange as it may seem, those big V8, high compression engines that everyone wants to unload could be the most efficient alcohol burners of all. The higher the compression ratio, the higher the efficiency of the alcohol burning engine. That means better mileage and more power. Small, low compression engines cannot utilize alcohol as well as the big V8's. Should this country ever change over to pure alcohol as a motor fuel, you just might see those huge V8's make a comeback.

Perhaps less known, but just as important, alcohol is a true dual fuel. Anyone who burns oil to heat their home, can just as easily burn alcohol! With just a slight, low-cost, modification of your oil-fired boiler or furnace you can burn alcohol to heat your home. And it doesn't even have to be pure alcohol. Anywhere from 150- to 190-proof alcohol (which con- tains some water) will actually create more heat than burning pure alco- hol. While much testing is still going on, it has already been discovered that alcohol as a heating fuel not only burns cleaner, but also burns with better combustion than oil--in a furnace designed to burn oil!

You might be starting to wonder why, if alcohol is so good, this country didn't just start right out with alcohol as a fuel, rather than petrol- eum-based fuels. The answer, as always, is money. It was cheaper to pump oil out of the ground and refine it than to distill alcohol from grain (at least on a mass scale), even when the distilled grain (mash) could later be used as cattle food. But this is not the only reason. You should keep in mind the times. The automobile was just getting its start in the late 1920s and early 30s. It was new, it was great, and it could give America a personal transportation system that was faster than the horse. The only problem was that there was a raging depression in the country. Hard cash was as scarce as hens' teeth. Banks were closing and folks were losing their homes, farms, and businesses. Millions were out of jobs. The government was wringing its hands and making promises it couldn't keep, as usual. But the sharp, big-money boys were into a good thing--oil! Everyone could see that the booming new automobile industry was going to take off. It was just a matter of time. Then all those new auto buyers would need oil and it's by-products, especially gasoline. All the big-money boys had to do was convince our government that gasoline was the motor fuel of the future--cheap motor fuel that would put everyone on wheels. But there was a fly in the ointment. A young engineer by the name of Henry Ford was manufacturing automobiles on an assembly line. While the politicians were promising a chicken in every pot, young Henry was thinking a Ford in every garage. He also had some very logical ideas about what motor fuel should be used for automobiles. He thought all cars should use alcohol. And he could list many reasons. Alcohol was safer than gasoline, it burned cleaner and, most important, it could be produced by our own farmers. Thereby providing them with a guaranteed cash crop and helping them keep their farms during bad times. And to give Mr. Ford credit, he put his money where his mouth was, and proceeded to produce cars with a dual carburetor that could use either gasoline or alcohol as fuel.

Well, the big-money boys couldn't take this lying down. They had all their chips sunk in oil. So the great oil versus alcohol battle was fought. Tests were made, contests between cars burning alcohol versus gasoline were held, Congressmen and Senators were called out, and money changed hands. When the smoke cleared, about the only thing proven was that big money had a way of getting politicians on their side. No big surprise to most Americans.

Today, we are watching another big fuel battle shape up. And just like yesteryear, a great deal of money is being spent to try and convince everyone that the only way to go is nuclear. We hear that nuclear power is clean, cheap, will last forever, and since the Three Mile Island nuclear accident, that it is safe. New controls have been installed, new safety measures have been provided, new and tougher regulations must be followed, and it won't happen again. Just don't live within 300 miles downwind of the things! It should not be hard to guess where the big-money boys are on this one. But once again, there is a fly in the ointment. A young man by the name of Michael Brown, who has spent the last seven years in carburetor design and fuel economy studies, has discovered that a diesel engine will run on (of all things) vegetable oil! Mr. Brown fired up a 600-horsepower Cummins diesel using common soybean oil. The diesel ran perfectly. Better yet, the soybean oil produced more power per pound than did diesel fuel! Best of all, no modifications were made to the big Cummins diesel for the test. Only the fuel was changed, which makes it entirely conceivable that all those folks driving diesel cars could just as well pour in vegetable oil for fuel! Almost enough to give oil companies nightmares!

Then there is the question that if vegetable oil will power diesel engines (with no modifications), why couldn't vegetable oil be used to power the electric companies' big diesel generators? And could it be possible that we could use it to heat our homes? Would it burn just as well in an oil furnace? Wouldn't that make the Arabs happy! Granted, at the moment vegetable oil costs more than diesel fuel. But for how long? And couldn't our government get together with the nation's farmers and put forth a major effort to produce both alcohol and vegetable oil at a reasonable price? Rather than pour billions of dollars into nuclear power plants that have somewhat shaky safety records, wouldn't it make more sense to build up our farmers, giving them a cash crop that they could count on every year, and keep our country's balance of payment problems on this side of the ocean while we have a fuel supply that we can count on every year? It made sense back in the 1920s and it makes sense now. Are we going to make the same mistakes all over again? We will if the big-money boys get their way. And how long before some Middle East oil producing nation gets mad enough at us to cut off their oil? What happens then, another war? Does America really want to take the risk when we can produce our own alternative fuels at home? We have the technology. We have the land and farmers to work the land. And we have the money (even knowing that a complete changeover will cost a bundle). But do we have the willpower? Will we all get actively involved and tell our Congressmen and Senators what we want for a change? If we don't, will our grandchildren, living in the shadow of a nuclear power plant, ever forgive us?

Just as important as the "dual fuels" is the Poor Man's super fuel, solar power. I have no doubt that sun power is the fuel of the future. Had our country made a major effort to explore the real potential of solar power twenty years ago, I sincerely doubt if we would face a fuel crisis today. Solar energy offers us an almost cost-free power source. As advances continue to be made in solar technology, we should see the cost of fuel and power drop back to a reasonable cost, but only if we can convince our government that this is where we want our research money spent. Otherwise, we will see our tax dollars literally poured into the pockets of the big-money boys. Every day you can see projections made as to how much oil will be imported into this country over the next few years, and projections as to how much oil we are using, versus how much is left in the ground. How about a projection on just how long our country can pour out billions of dollars for imported oil before going bankrupt! Two years? Five years? At the present rate of price increases along with our present rate of imported oil use, our beautiful, rich country could be bankrupt in less than five years! A crash effort must be made, right now! With a major effort our country could become almost totally fuel independent within five to ten years, but only if you get mad and raise a little hell with your government representatives. Sometimes they need to be reminded that the government serves the people, not the big-money boys. The future of our country is in YOUR hands!

The Poor Man

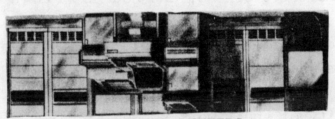

COMPUTER LETTERS

A well-known company recently sent out a large mailing of those "personalized" computer letters. The letter was signed by a Ms. Catherine Gibbs. The following is a letter received by the company responding to the computer letter:

Dear Ms. Gibbs:
What I like best about your letter, Ms. Gibbs, is the way that you keep calling me by my name in every other paragraph. Many of us suffer from crises of identity these days and it's always useful to be reminded at regular intervals who we really are. You are also kind enough, Ms. Gibbs, to keep mentioning the name of the street on which I live, which helps me to "get myself together." Since you know me so well, Ms. Gibbs, what are you doing tomorrow night after work, Ms. Gibbs?
Sincerely,

HUBCAPS ANONYMOUS
(Or, what you see
ain't necessarily
what you get!)

After we built our home here in Maryland, we realized that we lived
somewhat out in the boondocks. Although we lived between two great
cities--Baltimore, and the hot-air capital of the world, Washington, D.C.
--there was no public transportation to speak of. Ours was one of the
few rural areas left between the cities that hadn't yet been overbuilt
with housing developments and shopping centers, which is why we liked
it in the first place. The big disadvantage was that we had to rely
heavily on our own cars to go anywhere. After one long hike of about
eight miles to the nearest service station, I learned that one should
keep the family car in good repair. Otherwise, one could spend a lot of
time walking up lonely roads. Which is how I met Tiny.

Now Tiny, unlike his name implies, was not small. Tiny was, by anyone's
standards, huge. And I don't mean big, huge. I mean huge, huge. Like
King Kong huge! He stood at least six-foot-six, and seemed at least as
wide. He probably weighed in at a tad over 360 pounds. He was big, black
as the ace of spades, and bald as a bowling ball. He was also the best
auto mechanic that I ever saw. If it had four wheels and was called an
automobile, he could fix it. He had worked on everything from Model "A"
Fords to imported Mercedes-Benzes, and hadn't "lost a one yet" as he was
fond of saying. Besides his mechanical skills, he had another thing going
for him--a great sense of humor. He could laugh just as hard when the
joke was on him, as when it was on someone else. As a result, he and the
three young mechanics that worked for him enjoyed their work more than
most. And the quality of their work showed it. They always had a string
of cars lined up outside waiting for repairs.

The first time I met Tiny, I had walked into the shop to a roar of
laughter. There was this hugh black man standing by a shop bench tugging
at a wrench someone had spot-welded to the metal benchtop. Between roars
of laughter, he was making most unkind comments on the ancestry of anyone
who would weld a wrench to a benchtop. His three young mechanics were
all claiming innocence of the dirty deed and were all very busy working
while trying to stifle their laughter. He finally gave a giant tug on the

wrench and ripped it free of the benchtop. Turning around, he spotted me for the first time. "And what do you know about this?" he asked. Looking up at this man with arms the size of my legs and hands the size of Virginia hams, one of which held a big steel wrench under my nose, I really didn't quite know what to say. Finally, I came out with something like, "Friend, if I knew anything at all, I wouldn't be here right now." He looked me right in the eye, then burst out with another roar of laughter ending with "Right on!"

Later, after getting to know Tiny and his crew a lot better, I always made it a point to bring a cold six-pack of beer with me whenever I had to bring in the car. I found that this always assured me of fast service as Tiny would always take a break for a cold beer. He and his mechanics would gather around a workbench and make short work of the beer. Meanwhile, I would proceed to tell them what I thought was wrong with the car that I had brought in. Tiny would ask a few questions, think it over for a minute, then tell me what was really wrong with my car. When there was a difference of opinion, small bets were made and I would end up with four topnotch mechanics going over my car. While this was going on they would tell me the latest stories of who did what, to whom, and how they did it. Accompanied by much laughter.

One of Tiny's mechanics was an ignition and tune-up specialist. This young man had gone to a number of schools sponsored by various automobile manufacturers. He was also working his way through college for a degree in electrical engineering. This kid was sharp, and knew it. His only real problem was that sometimes he let his mouth run before he got his brain in gear. He was trying hard to impress Tiny with all his electrical knowledge and sometimes ended up putting some of the other guys down. This went on for the first month or so after Tiny hired him. It wasn't long before the other mechanics and Tiny got fed up with this nonsense. So they waited until this new mechanic got a hot tune-up job for an important customer. Tiny made it a point to stress just how good a customer this car owner (a doctor) was, and how important it was to keep him pleased, etc. The big buildup. The new man really got to work and made a big show of attaching electronic gear to the car's ignition to make sure that every little thing was just right. Of course everybody was just waiting until the job was complete, then they made up some excuse to get the young man away from the car for a few minutes. When he came back to the car and was just getting ready to shut the hood, Tiny sorta wandered over and said, "Why don't you start her up one more time and let's see what she sounds like?" The new man, eager to show off his skills to the boss, did just that. He hit the car's starter, expecting the engine to purr right to life. Instead, he heard a screaming, whistling noise like a falling bomb, then a huge explosion, and a gray cloud of smoke poured out from under the car's hood. Tiny watched all this without cracking a smile. He looked at the cloud of smoke, looked at the new young mechanic whose eyes were as wide as saucers, shook his head and slowly walked away. For the first time, the new man was speechless with shock, while everybody else in the shop was breaking up with laughter. Tiny had installed an old-time whistle bomb (a firecracker with a whistle) onto the car's ignition so that when the ignition switch was cut on, the bomb went off. They never had any more problems with this young mechanic telling them how good he was.

My next trip to Tiny's was on a very cold New Year's Eve. The temperature had dropped to nothing and the battery in my old car had given up the ghost. I had to jump start the car to get it running and then I drove directly over to Tiny's, stopping only to pick up a six-pack and leaving the engine running while I ran inside. When I finally reached Tiny's shop, there was this little guy, madder than a cat after a bath, jumping up and down in the middle of the shop floor. He was also about three sheets to the wind. Anyway, here he was jumping up in Tiny's face about a missing hubcap. I knew that he had to be half plastered, or crazy, seeing as how his head only reached slightly above Tiny's belt buckle. Tiny was taking it all very calmly. In fact, I suspect he was sort of enjoying this little guy's act. Seems the guy had been in the day before and bought a set of new tires for his expensive sports car. Now he was on his way to New York for the holiday, and discovered that one of his hubcaps was missing. He thought that either Tiny's boy had left the hubcap off, or had not put it on correctly and it had fallen off somewhere. He wanted a new hubcap, and he wanted it now! Everybody in the shop was frantically looking under things, on top of worktables, in corners, in storage bins, everywhere a missing hubcap could possibly hide. And the longer they looked, the madder the little man got. Somehow, he had convinced himself that he just had to have that hubcap in order to make it to New York. I tried to stay out of it and in the background, but the man saw me and just had to come over and tell me all of his troubles. He pointed out the tire with the missing hubcap on the driver's side, then proceeded to tell me how he wasn't leaving without that hubcap. Looking over his head, I noticed that Tiny had disappeared. Something that for someone as large as Tiny, was rather hard to do. I thought I heard a slight wrenching noise over by the man's car but didn't see anything. Meanwhile, the little guy in front of me was now into the price of hubcaps, and did I have any idea how much they cost? According to him, the hubcaps were the most expensive part of his car and, looking at his little car, I could believe it. Then Tiny suddenly reappeared from somewhere with a huge grin on his face. He had the missing hubcap. With a great show he snapped it in place on the rear wheel, giving it a couple of whacks with his giant paws. The little guy was all smiles. Now, he could make his trip to New York in style. He had his hubcap. Or so he thought.

As we gathered around Tiny's workbench and opened the cold beer, I asked Tiny where had he found the missing hubcap. He just grinned, took a swig of beer, and said that it was on the car all the time. What! How could that be, Tiny? He winked, and said it was on the right front tire. Slowly it sank in just what he had done. He had just switched the right front hubcap to replace the missing left rear hubcap, while the little guy was talking to me. Tiny said, "Did you notice we got him so mad that he was almost sober before he drove away." "Yep," I answered, "but that guy is going to be hopping mad when he gets to New York and discovers what you did." Tiny just grinned again and said, "No sweat, man, everybody knows that New Yorkers are notorious for stealing hubcaps."

## DO-IT-YOURSELF KINDLING

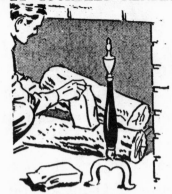

The do-it-yourselfer with a
fireplace in the home should
consider bagging all wood shav-
ings, sawdust, and small scraps
into small paper bags. The bags
of wood scraps make excellent
kindling for your fireplace or
wood stove.

## AX WEDGE SAFETY

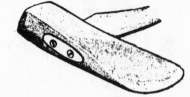

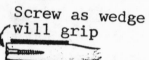

Wedge can
work loose        Screw as wedge
                  will grip

When your ax or hatchet
head works loose due to
a loose wedge (as it will
sooner or later) remove the
wedge and insert one or two
small flathead wood screws
for a good grip.

## THE POOR MAN'S DRAFT SNOOPER

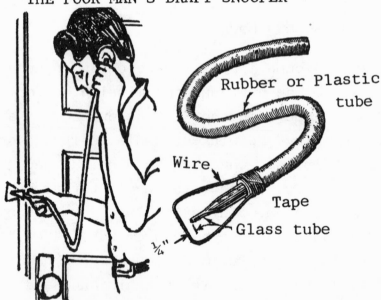

Every energy-concerned homeowner should have this little
goodie. And it's so simple to make. When in use, the whirls
and eddy currents set up in the glass tube when air blows
across the wire make it a most sensitive draft detector.
Just insert a glass eye-dropper tube into a length of rubber
or plastic tubing. Tape a piece of paper-clip wire bent as
shown, so that the horizontal part comes within ¼" of the
small hole in the glass tube. Put one end of the plastic tube
to your ear and pass the sensitive draft detector end near the
edge of a window or door. Normally inaudible tiny drafts become
howlings with every change of air velocity. Now, you can really
pinpoint those tiny drafts for fixing. You may be real surprised
at how many you find.

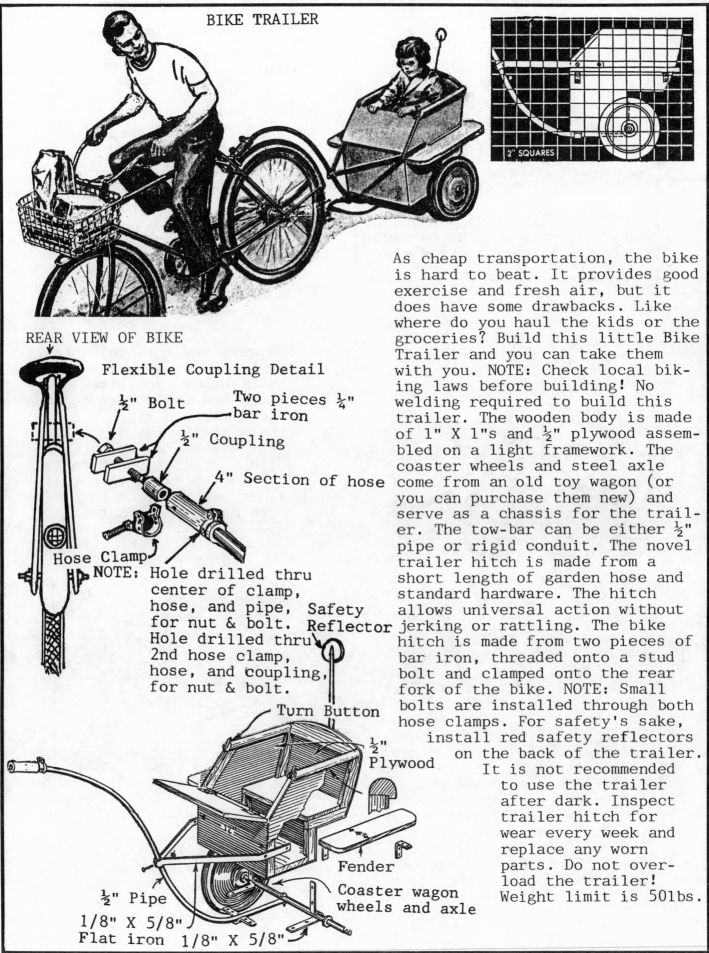

# BIKE TRAILER

2" SQUARES

REAR VIEW OF BIKE

## Flexible Coupling Detail

½" Bolt

Two pieces ¼" bar iron

½" Coupling

4" Section of hose

Hose Clamp

NOTE: Hole drilled thru center of clamp, hose, and pipe, for nut & bolt. Hole drilled thru 2nd hose clamp, hose, and coupling, for nut & bolt.

Safety Reflector

Turn Button

½" Plywood

Fender

Coaster wagon wheels and axle

½" Pipe

1/8" X 5/8"

Flat iron  1/8" X 5/8"

As cheap transportation, the bike is hard to beat. It provides good exercise and fresh air, but it does have some drawbacks. Like where do you haul the kids or the groceries? Build this little Bike Trailer and you can take them with you. NOTE: Check local biking laws before building! No welding required to build this trailer. The wooden body is made of 1" X 1"s and ½" plywood assembled on a light framework. The coaster wheels and steel axle come from an old toy wagon (or you can purchase them new) and serve as a chassis for the trailer. The tow-bar can be either ½" pipe or rigid conduit. The novel trailer hitch is made from a short length of garden hose and standard hardware. The hitch allows universal action without jerking or rattling. The bike hitch is made from two pieces of bar iron, threaded onto a stud bolt and clamped onto the rear fork of the bike. NOTE: Small bolts are installed through both hose clamps. For safety's sake, install red safety reflectors on the back of the trailer. It is not recommended to use the trailer after dark. Inspect trailer hitch for wear every week and replace any worn parts. Do not overload the trailer! Weight limit is 50lbs.

46

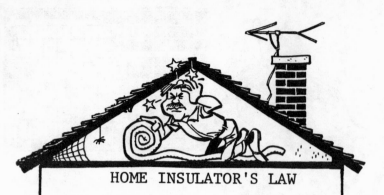

## HOME INSULATOR'S LAW

The insulation that you paid thru the nose and busted your budget for, goes on sale next week. You know, you can't win!

## MINI RIDER SEAT

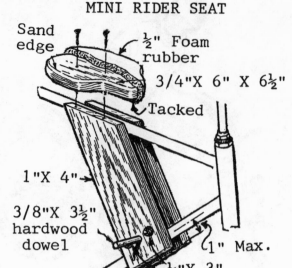

As more and more folks take to bikes for both exercise and economy, sometimes a youngster would like to go along for the ride. Build the Mini Rider Seat as shown and they can enjoy the ride with you. Be sure to install the wooden dowel foot rests as it makes the child's ride much more comfortable.

## POOR MAN'S HOT LUNCHBOX

Having done shift work for more years than I care to remember, I did get tired of cold sandwiches. Then I discovered that three Pyrex rectangular containers would fit neatly into my old metal lunchbox. By drilling a 7/16" hole in one end of the cover for a 1/8" pipe nipple and adding a ceramic socket, which was wired into a cord and plug, I could turn my lunchbox into a neat "Hot Lunchbox." A 150-watt bulb plugged in 30 minutes before lunch would give me piping hot meats, vegetables, and soups. NOTE: Don't forget and leave any napkins, or paper or plastic wrapped sandwiches in the box when heating. It could start a fire!

## PEDAL POWER PARKER

With all of the folks riding bikes nowadays, you might experience bike parking problems. The simple device shown above is just a notched board attached with a pivot to a handy corner or wooden post.

## POOR MAN'S EL CHEAPO ATTIC INSULATION

With the cost of heating your home going through the roof, any extra added attic insulation can help save you a bundle of bucks. Along with everything else, the price of home insulation materials has also gone through the roof. But without added insulation in your attic, your heat will go through the roof! Not really very funny when the cost of heating your home can drive you

into bankruptcy. But have no fear, the cure is here! The Poor Man's El Cheapo Attic Insulation. So cheap that anyone can afford it, and so simple to install that anyone can install it. Better yet, it will help keep you cooler in the summer, and much warmer in the winter. Best of all, the total cost is less than 4¢ per square foot. How's that for a penny squeezer!

The Poor Man's El Cheapo Insulation Material is plain old aluminum foil, available at your local super market in 18" rolls. The 18" width is just right for attic installation allowing for a small overlap along the edges. We can recommend Reynolds (heavy duty) aluminum foil. The foil surfaces will reflect heat away from your ceilings in the summer, and reflect heat back down in the winter, not allowing heat to escape thru your attic. Aluminum foil also acts as a vapor barrier keeping your existing insulation from absorbing moisture and losing much of its insulating value. Follow the instructions given below, and you will be amazed at the savings on your next heating bill.

1. Determine square feet of aluminum foil needed.
2. Obtain tacks or a staple gun with staples.
3. Tack or staple the foil across the joists in your attic with the dull side facing down, and reflective side facing up. Overlap foil at junctures.

IMPORTANT: Start from point farthest away from entrance and be sure to take all precautions called for when working in your attic. For example: Be aware of electric wiring; do not tack into electric wires; do not walk between joists; do not use open flames for light; do not use unsafe steps or ladders.

4. DO NOT BLOCK GABLE VENTS, LOUVERS OR EAVE VENTS.
5. To insulate living space in an attic, staple or tack foil across collar beams, down rafters and kneewall studs, and along ceiling joists to the wall plate. Leave at least 3/4" air space between foil and roof sheathing for full insulating value.

48

## AX SHOCK ABSORBER

Rubber strip

Nail a strip of old
auto tire casing just
behind the bit and
your ax handle will
not become "chewed up"
when splitting wood
and kindling.

## FOR YOUR SAFETY'S SAKE

Most gamblers will tell you that
if you can cut the odds against
you by 50% you have a good bet.
The National Highway Traffic Safety
Administration has found in a new
study that cars equipped with a
high mounted brake light, located
just under the back window, had
more than 50% fewer rear-end acci-
dents than vehicles without the
added light. The rear window brake
lights are at close to eye level,
making them easier for a following
driver to see when you apply your
brakes. Any auto accessory store
carries spare 12-volt red lights,
which can be wired into your car's
existing taillight system at low
cost. This is well worth the small
investment.

## WOOD STORAGE RACK

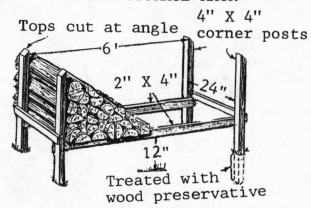

Tops cut at angle    4" X 4"
corner posts
6'
2" X 4"    24"
12"
Treated with
wood preservative

Pesky little critters like mice
just love to make their home in
woodpiles. You can eliminate
this problem along with allowing
better air circulation around
your cut wood by building the
simple wood rack as shown above.

Occupational hazard for the
Internal Revenue Service agent.
A nose problem!

```
ENERGY SAVER'S LAW

The energy that you save
today will most surely
go up in price tomorrow.
```

## CUT HEATING BILLS BY UP TO 25%

If you heat your home with either natural gas or heating oil, and your furnace is located inside your home, you can easily cut your heating bill from 12 to 25%! It's as simple as installing the air intake project (A) shown below. It works like this: Your furnace--either oil or natural gas fired--requires from 1,200 to 2,000 cubic feet of air for proper combustion. All of this air must come from somewhere. Usually, it comes from inside the home. This is air that you have already paid to have heated. This heated air is burned in the combustion chamber of your furnace in the combustion process and then sent out the chimney. Almost like burning your money! Since this burned air must be replaced, it is sucked from around doors and windows (anywhere in the house), creating drafts. When running, your furnace sucks in your already heated air, along with cold outside air to replace the heated air. But your furnace really doesn't care about the temperature of the air it uses in the combustion process. It can work equally well with cold air or the already heated inside air. So why not let it use cold outside air by installing a simple outside air intake pipe and lead it directly to your furnace. Your furnace will never know the difference but you certainly will! The savings in fuel could astonish you. No adjustments to your furnace are required.

Project (B) can greatly increase the comfort level in your basement by drawing cold air from floor level and sending it up the chimney with the smoke. Plus, if you have not installed project (A) above, you will use slightly less warm air in the combustion process of your furnace, for a small fuel savings. Some adjustment to your furnace may be needed.

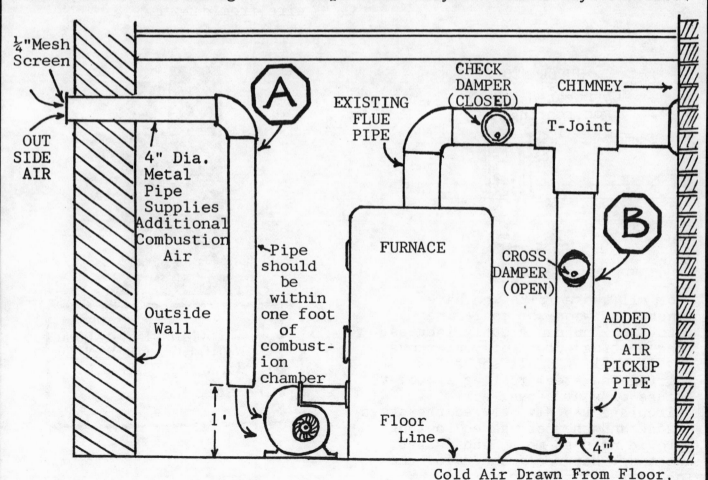

Cold Air Drawn From Floor.

## WAX LOG KINDLING

Those wax and sawdust logs
sold for fireplaces will
last longer and start a fire
just as fast if you first cut
them into about ½" steaks,
break into small chunks, and
use with paper kindling. They
will start a roaring wood log
fire in your fireplace in no
time. Used in small chunks,
they can also be used to start
log fires in wood stoves. About
one half a "steak" broken into
chunks will do it. Never use
an entire wax log in a wood
stove. It could give you a lot
bigger fire than you want!

Installing a few sections of
6" stovepipe in your fireplace,
and setting a small electric
fan to circulate air through
it, will almost double the
usable heat output of your
fireplace. The stovepipe is
assembled as shown, and is
positioned so that the flames
will pass both behind and in
front of it. (Can be hung with
wire from damper.)

## SUPER STOVE

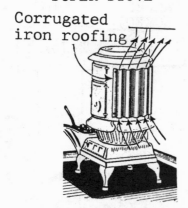

For all those folks who have
installed wood- or coal-fired
stoves. You can greatly increase
the heating output of your stove
by installing small sheets of
corrugated steel roofing around the
sides of your stove. Air will
circulate rapidly between the stove
sides and the corrugated roofing,
providing both more, and faster,
heating. Not recommended for the
new air-tight stoves.

THE ONLY THING WRONG
WITH THIS COUNTRY
IS WASHINGTON, D.C.

The Poor Man

## STOVEPIPE TIPS

### DOWNDRAFT TILTING CAP

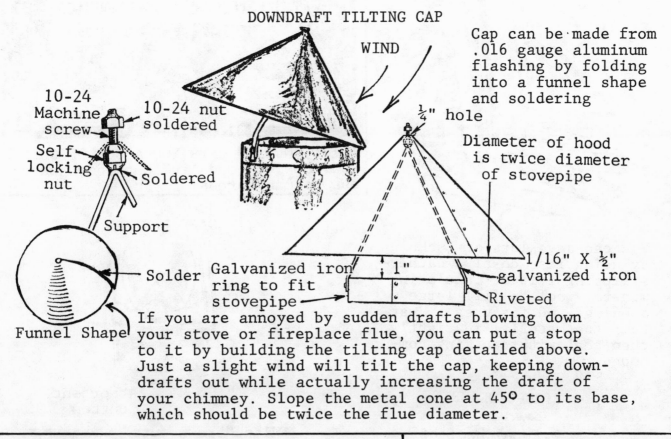

WIND

10-24 Machine screw

10-24 nut soldered

Self locking nut

Soldered

Support

Solder

Funnel Shape

¼" hole

Cap can be made from .016 gauge aluminum flashing by folding into a funnel shape and soldering

Diameter of hood is twice diameter of stovepipe

Galvanized iron ring to fit stovepipe

1"

1/16" X ½" galvanized iron

Riveted

If you are annoyed by sudden drafts blowing down your stove or fireplace flue, you can put a stop to it by building the tilting cap detailed above. Just a slight wind will tilt the cap, keeping down-drafts out while actually increasing the draft of your chimney. Slope the metal cone at 45º to its base, which should be twice the flue diameter.

### POOR MAN'S CRIMPING TOOL

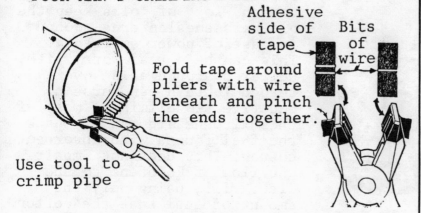

Adhesive side of tape

Bits of wire

Fold tape around pliers with wire beneath and pinch the ends together.

Use tool to crimp pipe

Couple stovepipe or light-gauge ducts by using this simple homemade tool. It is capable of crimping sheet metal up to .064" in thickness. Make from a pair of mechanics pliers, a few finishing brads or wire, cut to ½" lengths. Stick them to strips of adhesive tape as shown, then wrap around jaws of the pliers.

### STOVEPIPE CLEANING BAGS

Paper Bag

You can avoid much extra work when taking stove-pipes down for cleaning by closing the ends with paper bags and rubber bands. This keeps soot from spilling all over your floors while moving the pipes out-side for cleaning.

## SAVE CAULKING MONEY

THIS, AND 35¢ GETS YOU A CUP OF COFFEE
Wow! How do we do it? Eat your heart
out, Neiman-Marcus!

You can save lots of bucks
by using less costly weather-
stripping felt or insulating
mineral wool to fill large
openings and fissures.  Just
tamp the material in tightly,
then seal with caulking compound.

## SAFE LANTERN

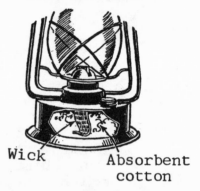

Wick          Absorbent
                 cotton

With "brown outs" and power
outages becoming more and more
common, lots of folks keep the
old kerosene lanterns around
in case of power emergency.
This can be a real worry with
children around as an over-
turned lantern can cause a
bad fire. To eliminate most of
this fire hazard, simply pack
the fuel founts with absorbent
cotton. This does not impair
the flow of kerosene to the
wick. Fill, using only the
amount of fuel that the cotton
can absorb.

## FIREPLACE CRANE

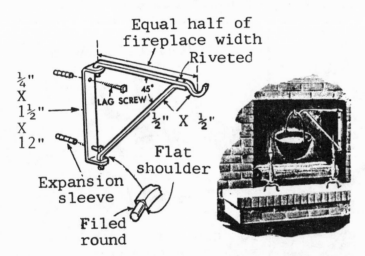

Equal half of
fireplace width
Riveted
¼"
X
1½"
X
12"
45°
LAG SCREW
½" X ½"
Flat
shoulder
Expansion
sleeve
Filed
round

As in the days of old, your fireplace
can do a lot more than just give you
heat.  Install a pivoted crane to one
side and you can heat water, soup, stew,
or anything that you can get into a pot.
A flat steel bracket with its ends bent
outwards is drilled and bolted to the
fireplace wall with lag screws turned
into expansion sleeves. The swinging
part of the crane is made of two pieces
of square ½" steel rod, long enough to
locate a hook-shaped end of the upper
piece in the center of the fireplace.

Hammer Down
Inflation
Do-It-Yourself

## THE KOREAN CONTRIBUTION

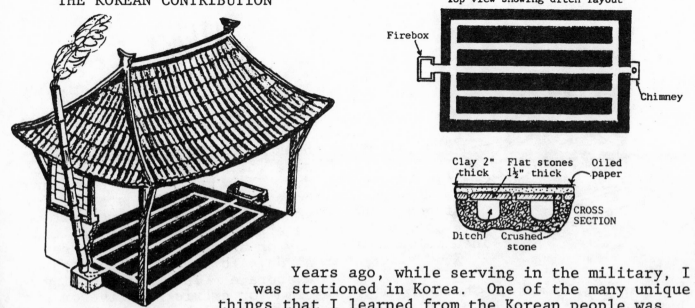

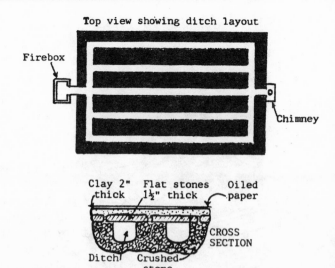

Top view showing ditch layout

Firebox

Chimney

Clay 2" thick   Flat stones 1½" thick   Oiled paper

CROSS SECTION

Ditch   Crushed stone

Years ago, while serving in the military, I was stationed in Korea. One of the many unique things that I learned from the Korean people was how their "radiant heating" home heating system worked. It is a low-cost system, well over 2,000 years old, that keeps a home toasty warm on bitter cold winter nights. What is completely unique about their radiant heating system is that it uses the smoke and hot gases to provide heat. It does not use the stove or firebox, which is usually located outside the rear of the house. The builder first digs out the floor of his new home to a depth of 1½'. He then fills his dugout floor with small rocks and stones. Next, he lays out, and digs ditches about 3' apart in the stones. He connects these ditches with his firebox at one end of the house, and his chimney at the other. Over these ditches he lays slabs of flat stone. Over the stone, he smooths a layer of mud about 2" thick. Over the mud, he lays heavy oiled paper. In operation, his chimney draws the smoke and hot gases through the ditches, warming the floor and radiating heat throughout the home. This method seems to spread the heat much more evenly than many modern-day heating systems.

A more modern version of this method could be a perfect low-cost alternative for small homes, cottages, or even log cabins. The plan below shows how radiant heating could be utilized using an (inside) drum stove. (Almost any stove would work.) By digging a sort of mini split-level area for the stove, it could then be used for cooking and heating. In building, you would lay hardware cloth and tar paper over the ditches before pouring the reinforced concrete floor. The tar paper would burn off with the first use of the stove, but, if only strips were used to cover the ditches, there should be no problem. A special "high heat" concrete may have to be used for the floor. A high, well-drawing chimney is a must!

TOP VIEW

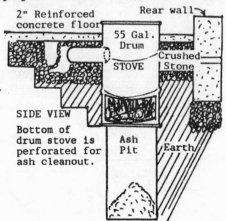

2" Reinforced concrete floor   Rear wall   55 Gal. Drum   STOVE   Crushed Stone

SIDE VIEW

Bottom of drum stove is perforated for ash cleanout.   Ash Pit   Earth

54

## POOR MAN'S STOVE BASE

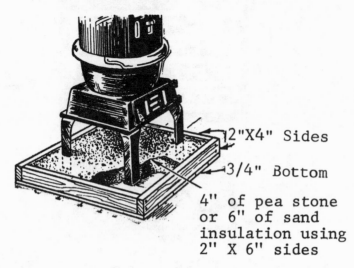

2"X4" Sides

3/4" Bottom

4" of pea stone or 6" of sand insulation using 2" X 6" sides

You can easily make a "heat-proof" base for your stove by building a wooden box at least 4" wider than the base diameter of your stove and filling it level with pea stone, washed gravel, or even beach pebbles. If sand is used as insulation, box must be enlarged to hold 6" of sand.

## BURNING BRICK

Soak an ordinary brick in kerosene for 48 hours and allow to dry. You now have an emergency heat supply or fire starter for your fireplace or stove. It can be extinguished and re-ignited a day or so later. It takes several days for the kerosene to evaporate. The total burning time for a brick is five or six hours. Small brick chunks soaked in kerosene and stored in a sealed coffee can make an excellent fire starter for campers.

## OLD-TIME TOASTER/ROASTER

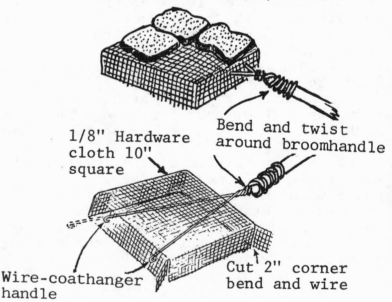

1/8" Hardware cloth 10" square

Bend and twist around broomhandle

Wire-coathanger handle

Cut 2" corner bend and wire

With "brown outs" and possible power failures, the Old-Time Toaster/Roaster could make a comeback. Excellent for use with fireplace or stove. Just make an open box of 1/8" hardware cloth and attach a 3' section of broom handle. Use the back side for toast and the flip side (open box) for hamburgers, fried potatoes, and hot dogs. Add a screen top for popcorn.

### LAW OF TAXES

Tax the rich fairly and you create jobs. Tax the poor unjustly and you create hardship. Tax the middle-class for all of it, and you create a new revolution!

# THE ELEPHANT'S TRUNK

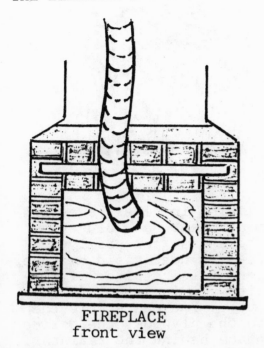

FIREPLACE
front view

A fireplace can be a most useful item in your home. It can help keep you warm in the winter, and modified as shown, it can help keep you cool in the summer.

By cutting a ¼" sheet of plywood to fit tightly over your fireplace opening, and cutting a circular opening near the top center of the plywood sheet, you can install what we call the "Elephant's Trunk." This is really a flexible plastic hose usually used as a hot air exhaust hose for home clothes dryers. (Available at most local hardware and Sears stores.)

This flexible plastic hose is attached to a small section of metal stovepipe which is stuck through the hole you cut through the sheet of plywood. The other end of the plastic hose is attached about 4" from the ceiling with a cup hook and wire. A small fan is installed behind the plywood sheet in the fireplace and aimed upwards as much as possible. The chimney damper is opened all the way to allow hot air to escape up the chimney.

NOTE: If you have another fireplace upstairs using the same chimney, don't use the Elephant's Trunk method downstairs, as it will blow soot all over the place.

In operation, the fan behind the plywood sheet in the fireplace sucks hot air from your ceiling, through the plastic pipe and exhausts it out the chimney. It does the same job as an attic fan at much less cost and work. While it might look a little weird in your fireplace (kids love it!), you will be amazed at how fast it can help cool your house down on a hot summer day, or night!

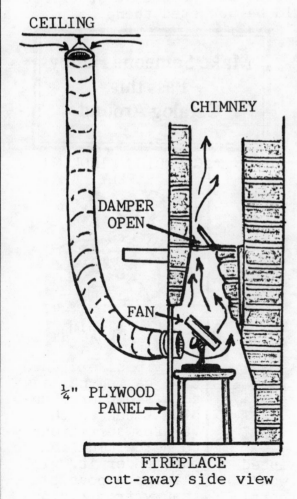

FIREPLACE
cut-away side view

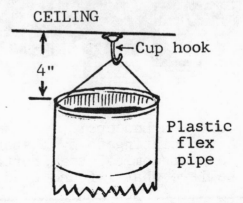

## POOR MAN'S DOGHOUSE HEATER

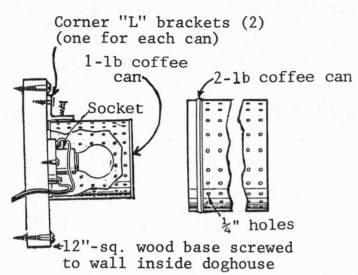

Corner "L" brackets (2)
(one for each can)

1-lb coffee
can

Socket

2-lb coffee can

¼" holes

12"-sq. wood base screwed
to wall inside doghouse

Now, here is something that I really
know all about, having spent a lot
of time in one myself. (Just ask my
wife!)  You can keep your dog warm
and comfortable on wet cold nights
by installing this low-cost, simple
heater.  Just drill or punch ¼" holes
all around both coffee cans and
install around a 40-watt light bulb
and fixture as shown. By using two
cans, you cut down the light to a
warm glow; by using the protected
light bulb, you provide an evenly
radiated heat.

## RADIATING RADIATORS

Folks living in older homes and
apartments that have old steam
heat radiators, can easily
increase the heat yield by covering a cut-to-size piece of plywood with aluminum foil (shiny
side out).  You can staple the
foil to the plywood, then slide
into place behind the radiator.
The foil acts as a heat reflector
bouncing out heat that otherwise
would be pocketed there.

### Make Someone Happy
### Pass this
### Catalog Around

Dear Ann Landers:
After hinting to my husband that I wanted
some economical transportation, you won't
believe what I found tied in our carport!

## CHOPPING KINDLING SAFELY

A strip of old auto
tire casing nailed
to a stump or chop-
ping block so that
it arcs sufficiently
to allow kindling to
pass under it, will
eliminate possible
injury from flying
cut pieces.

## COOLING TWO ROOMS WITH ONE WINDOW AIR CONDITIONER

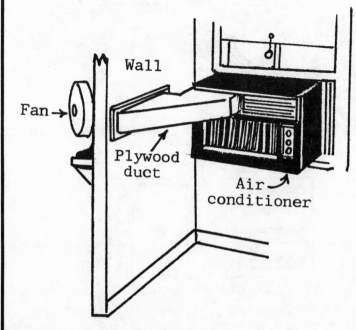

A small bedroom air conditioner that is located near a room dividing wall can usually cool two rooms almost as well as one. It might take a little longer, but it sure is cheaper than buying another air conditioner.

By building a simple ¼" plywood duct and installing it as shown, half of the cool air output from the window air conditioner is diverted through the dividing wall into the next room.

A small fan located just below the duct outlet in the next room will help circulate the cool air.

In cutting the duct opening through the wall, try to locate it so that it falls between the wall studs. The duct should be kept as short as possible for good air flow without loss. Make a cardboard pattern to obtain an exact fit. The wall opening is made slightly larger than the duct, then trim is applied around it on both sides of the wall.

## KEEP YOUR AIR CONDITIONER COOL

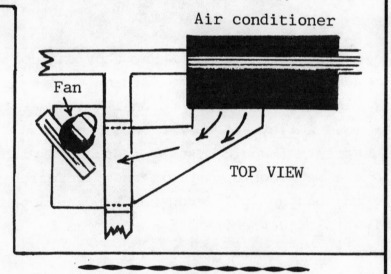

While it might sound a little nutty, if you will keep your window, or thru-the-wall air conditioner out of direct sun with an awning or plywood sunshade it will both increase its operating efficiency and lower the operating cost.

**One
Do-It-Yourselfer
is worth
Three
Can't-Do-It's!**

## TV TORNADO WATCH

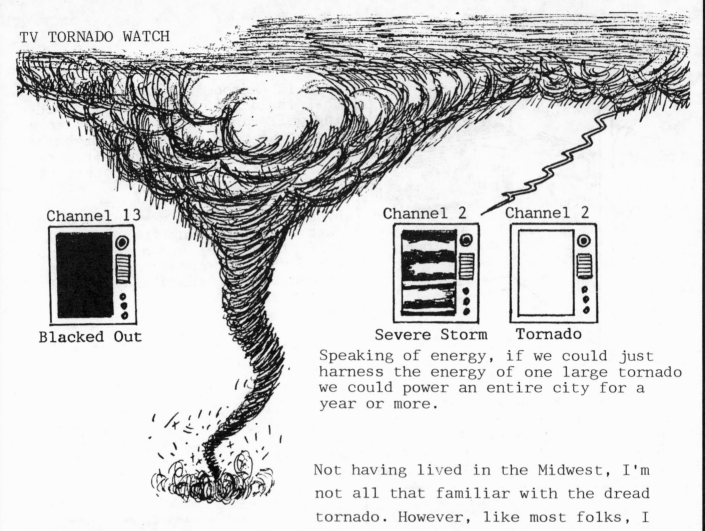

Channel 13

**Blacked Out**

Channel 2

**Severe Storm**

Channel 2

**Tornado**

Speaking of energy, if we could just harness the energy of one large tornado we could power an entire city for a year or more.

Not having lived in the Midwest, I'm not all that familiar with the dread tornado. However, like most folks, I have seen the damage that they can do from watching the TV and quite honestly, I hope that viewing this whirling disaster on the TV is as close as I ever get to one. We do get them in our state (Maryland) once in a while, but so far (knock on wood) none has come whirling down our street. I would just as soon stick with our nice, calm hurricanes. They are bad enough. In doing some research on another project, I happened to read an article on how you can actually use your TV set as a tornado warning device. And I don't mean by just listening to the weather forecast.

It seems that a gentleman in Des Moines, Iowa, by the name of Newton Weller, did a great deal of tornado research a few years back. He came up with an amazing discovery. Just by watching a blacked-out Channel 2 on your TV set, you can tell when a tornado is near your location. The blacked-out Channel 2 screen will turn bright (white) when a tornado is down in your area. When the screen turns white, the distance of the tornado from you can be anywhere from very close, to twenty or more miles away. Usually it is within five to ten miles away when picked up on your TV screen, depending upon whether you have an indoor or outdoor antenna. Since a tornado hops, skips, and jumps very fast, when that TV screen turns white, it's time to move directly to a shelter. Don't bother turning the TV off, just git up and go! If it's really close, your electric power will most probably go out before you can pull the plug anyway. Hopefully, you will have a flashlight at hand, and can grab your family, while making great haste to shelter. Don't let anyone stop to look out a window: flying glass can kill you. And don't run outside in the rain and wind to look for the thing. You could get blown away.

You will probably know beforehand if a tornado watch is in effect. Our weather service has gotten pretty good at forecasting these things. The radio or TV will broadcast warnings if there is enough time. And that, dear friends, is the catch. Tornadoes move so fast that they can be in your area before anyone is aware of it. It is usually part of a very severe storm with high winds, rain, and hail. The "funnel" of the tornado usually forms at the rear of the storm, most generally in the southwest corner of the storm cloud. The "funnel" can climb to 15 or 20,000 feet into the storm cloud. Here it is connected to what is known as the pulse generator. The pulse generator is a spiraling force of lightning revolving around a vacuum core. This generates the electrical radiation that triggers your TV channel 2. Mr. Weller discovered that the 55-megacycle band (Channel 2) is the nearest TV band to the electrical frequency of the pulse generator of a tornado. This is why this method of tornado warning is called the "Weller Method" named after its discoverer. This is not theory. The method works on killer tornados and has been proven many times. As always, there is a kicker! Some scientists don't believe that all tornadoes have this built-in pulse generator. In which case the TV tornado warning would not always work. The controversy may one day be settled, but for now, you pays your money and you takes your choice.

Mr. Weller's method works like this: First, you turn on your TV set when you suspect a tornado is in your area. You switch the channel selector to Channel 13 (because Channel 13 is a 211-megacycle frequency and outside the range of tornado electrical radiation). You now turn down the brightness control until Channel 13 is nearly blacked out. If you wait to turn down the brightness control on Channel 2, you could unwittingly turn down the brightness too far and darken out a real tornado warning which might already be showing on Channel 2. This is possible to do on some TV sets. Once you have Channel 13 nearly dark, then switch to Channel 2. You should see the same nearly dark screen. You may see some intermittent wide white bands which fade slowly. This means that you are watching a severe storm. The horizontal streaks are lightning. Should the screen turn ghostly white, that's it--take shelter! A tornado is most definitely in your area. You may have five minutes, or five seconds to get to shelter.

From my own experience, I'd advise you to believe it when you see that screen go white. About three weeks after accidently reading about the "Weller Method" I had a chance to find out for myself how well it works. We had a severe thunderstorm in the area--not at all unusual during mid-summer in our neck of the woods. I was busy working down in our basement and had my police/fire-scanner radio on and was wondering if our power was going to go out as it usually did during a bad storm. I heard our county police dispatcher announce that a tornado watch had just been issued by the weather service. Bingo, I thought, I'll just give Mr. Weller's TV tornado warning idea a workout. So, I switched on a color TV and went through the drill of first switching to Channel 13 and dark-ening the screen, then switching to Channel 2 (which was broadcasting a program) and sat watching a dark screen and listening to the program. My poor wife came down the steps and must have thought I had finally flipped out, sitting in the dark watching a dark TV screen. We were picking up a lot of static and an occasional broad white lightning streak across the screen. I had only been sitting four or five minutes when the entire screen turned ghostly white and as best I can remember I lost the sound. I sat in a state of shock not really believing what I was seeing--that ghostly white screen staring back at me. Then, like a dummy I decided to go out our back door and see if I could really see anything. The wind was up around forty or fifty miles an hour and blowing a driving rain. I got soaked to the skin and didn't see a thing but dark clouds and rain. I got very lucky. A tornado had touched down less than eight miles from our home. It was on the evening news, and next day the news-paper had pictures of the damage. Praise the Lord, no one was hurt--just property damage.

The Weller Method will work on either a black and white or most color TV sets. If you are on cable TV you must disconnect the cable from the back

61

of the set and connect the built-in antenna. It will work with either an inside or outside antenna. It will work even if there is a program being broadcast on either Channel 13 or Channel 2--in which case you will get the sound of the program along with static.

Taking Shelter. The old Boy Scout motto "Be Prepared" still makes a lot of sense, especially nowadays when most everything can be knocked out with an electrical power failure. If you live in a tornado area you probably already know the drill. But, for those who don't know, here is what is recommended: If at home, go to your underground storm cellar or your basement. Go to a corner of your basement and take cover under a sturdy workbench or table. Make sure that there are no heavy appliances on the floor above your head. If your home has no basement, take cover under heavy furniture on the ground floor, in the center part of the house. Stay away from windows and doors because, if the thing comes close, everything is going to take off flying. Do not remain in a mobile home if a tornado is approaching. Take cover elsewhere. If at work in an office building, go to the basement or to a small room such as a closet, on a lower floor. If driving in open country and there isn't time to drive away, or if walking, take cover and lie flat in the nearest depression, such as a ditch, culvert, excavation, or ravine. Crouch as low as possible making the smallest possible target of yourself, cover your eyes, and pray!

And I pray that no one reading this will ever have to use it. May all your tornadoes miss you by miles. Also, please keep in mind that the Weller Method is still not considered foolproof. According to the experts, a sneaky tornado could still sneak up on you--one that doesn't have a pulse generator--and your screen won't turn white. Until more is known, take all tornado warnings very seriously. Meanwhile, our heartfelt thanks to Mr. Weller for at least showing us how to get some warning.

If you would like more information on tornadoes and the Weller Method, you can send for a new book published by a friend of ours titled:
TORNADO-WISE! By Vincent Luciani
Price: $3.95 plus $1.00 postage.
From: Cologne Press, Box 682,
Cologne, NJ 08213

This book is well researched and will bring you right up to date on all information in this field. It also has a questionnaire allowing you to participate in a valuable public service. Your input could help save lives!

JEZEBEL

My first automobile was a 1931 Model "A" Ford. I had paid 150 hard-earned bucks for her and she was beautiful, as only your first car can be. She was used, of course, as only a Model "A" can be used by its hundred or so previous owners, most of whom were of high-school age. She was full of dents and dings, and the two front fenders had a lot of paint missing from too many close calls. But there was no rust to be found. She had originally started out as a four-door sedan, but somewhere along her rocky road there had been a serious rear-end collision. The body of the car from the windshield back had been completely rebuilt of wood. This gave her the rather odd appearance of a square box on wheels. Then add to this the fact that she had no roof, and you can understand her rather odd appearance. She was a completely unique four-door convertible. Only, with her new wooden body, she didn't have four doors. Matter of fact, she didn't have any doors. You just sort of hopped on the running board and climbed over the side to get in. Sorta like climbing into the first story window of a house. Speaking of windows, she didn't have any of those either--just the glass windshield, which did make riding in her a little breezy, especially in the wintertime. And since she had no top, not even a canvas convertible top, you did tend to get a bit wet if caught driving in a rainstorm. It also made for some interesting wintertime problems. She was the only car I ever owned where you had to shovel snow out of the car before shoveling the car out of the snow. Another interesting little feature was that she had no seats. Whoever had rebuilt her body had neglected to reinstall her seats. But have no fear, some ingenious soul had installed some very good wooden orange crates for seats. They were quite comfortable for short trips. But for long trips (like around the block) they did become somewhat hard. One had to be, shall we say, well upholstered in the right place for long trips. Otherwise, she would jolt your brains out! Now she did have her minor faults, but what she lacked in class, she more than made up for in driving thrills. In fact, every drive was a thrill because you never knew what was going to happen. While the engine was sound and she ran like a top, there was a minor problem with the voltage regulator. It would not charge the battery. We could never get it to work and since the car was so old, a new part was out of the question. Like clockwork, every two weeks the battery would go dead. To remedy this problem we simply kept several spare batteries with one always on a battery charger. When the one in the car (located under the driver's orange-crate seat) went dead, we just swapped it with a fully charged one. Our battery charger, which was almost as old as the car, did not have an automatic cutoff switch. You just left the battery charging for eight hours then tried to remember to unplug the thing. Of course, the day finally came that we forgot all about a charging battery. We left the charger plugged in for a week, twenty-four hours a day. Believe me, that was one well-charged battery! But it didn't seem to hurt it any. I inspected it carefully before installing it back under the driver's seat, hit the starter and Wham! She started that old engine in a flash. On this particular day, a friend and I had skipped school. We had spent the day sort of loafing around as teenagers will do on a fine spring day. Along about three in the afternoon we decided to drive over to our high school and pick up some friends after school let out. Our high school was located at the top of a long, steep hill. We arrived at the bottom of this hill just as school was letting out and kids were starting to stream out across the road and down the hill. We were about midway up the hill when I shifted back into second gear, and it happened. Our super-charged battery exploded! It just blew up under my orange-crate driver's seat with a loud Bam! You never saw two kids abandon ship so fast. But I did remember to yank on the emergency brake as I dove over the side of the car. The loud explosion and the sight of us bailing out attracted some attention, and before long we were surrounded by a crowd of kids all wanting to know what happened. As I was trying to explain that the battery had blown up, I noticed that it was getting just a little breezy around my legs. Looking down, I found that my jeans were slowly disintegrating around my ankles. Little pieces of denim material were dropping around my feet. When the battery had exploded under my seat, battery acid had been blown all over the back of my pants legs. With a hundred kids standing around, and at least half of them teenage girls, I beat a hasty retreat back up the hill and into the school's restroom. After discarding my air conditioned jeans I carefully washed my legs down with water. With nothing else to wear, I ended up having to wear an old gym towel wrapped around my waist, much to the delight of my laughing friends. Needless to say, I never heard the end of it. That very same day, using bright reflective tape, I lettered the back bumper of my car with her new name. Jezebel! She was certainly no lady, but you never had a dull moment with her, either!

THE POOR MAN

GAS SAVER

Empty one-pound coffee cans make an excellent way of disposing of used oil filters when changing your car's oil. Most filters will fit into the coffee can, then just slip the plastic lid back on and you have a clean way to keep dirty oil from running through your trash. When installing a new oil filter on your car, first fill it half full with new oil, and it will give your engine instant lubrication when started. Plus, you will be able to tell immediately if it's going to leak.

Make it a point to fillup your buggy after dark when the temperature has dropped and you can save from 2½ to 5 percent on your gas bill. Gasoline actually shrinks as it gets colder. Expands as it gets warmer.

WANTED: Dynamic, young executive to manage low cost housing project. Must be experienced!

# Lawn & Garden

The lawn and garden projects shown below are not available in <u>this</u> catalog. They are available in our self-published Poor Man's Catalog #5.

Look out! Here comes old Shake and Bake again!

I can't think of anything I'd rather be doing!

## THE MANTIS CONNECTION

Not too many years ago, the Praying Mantis
was being advertised as the gardener's dream.
Here was a bug that would chase down and hunt
garden pests, while almost eating his weight
in amphids, beetles, and other assorted bad
bugs each day. And the Mantis certainly looked the part. When full-grown he could range in
size from three to five inches and was
equipped with long, powerful front legs com-
plete with sharp spines for holding its prey. Unfortunately, as later
research proved, this evil-looking fellow is way overbilled. He doesn't
eat his weight in bad bugs each day because he doesn't actually hunt the
bad guys, but sits waiting for one to crawl or fly by. The little Lady-
bug easily outperforms the Praying Mantis as a predator. What had happened was that the advertising copywriter types had taken a good look at
his spectacular appearance, and credited him with everything from eating
his way through hordes of bad bugs, to scaring rabbits out of the garden
for you. But this advertising copy sold a lot of Mantis egg cases to
happy gardeners across the country. Each egg case contained from 1 to
300 hungry little mantises ready to pop out in mid-spring and eat everything that moved in your garden. According to the advertising copy, all
the gardener had to do in the fall was place the Mantis egg cases in
spots where the little critters would do the most good, come spring.

One crisp fall day while out walking in some of the fields around our
housing development, I was pleasantly surprised to discover (of all
things) Praying Mantis egg cases in some of the tall, dried out reeds in
the field. These foamlike, yellowish-colored clusters were attached near
the tops of the dried reeds. Usually the egg case was formed right around
the reed stem making them quite easy to remove without damaging the egg
case. During my walk, I gathered a good half-dozen egg cases with ease.
Once back home, I selected likely looking spots around our house and
garden to place the egg cases. I saved one to show the family when I
went back inside. Our eldest son (fourteen at the time, and always looking for ways to make a buck) took great interest in the little Praying
Mantis egg case, asking where I had found them, and how much they sold

for in the mail order catalogs. So I wasn't surprised to learn the very next day that our son and some of his friends were out in the fields after school, looking for Mantis egg cases. Before long they were going door to door, selling egg cases to home owners and gardeners. They covered every home in our development and sold quite a few. Encouraged, one of the kids drew up a sales brochure complete with a wicked looking picture of a Praying Mantis. Using our little duplicating machine they printed up several hundred copies. Now, if the home owner wasn't at home when they called with their sales pitch, they left the sales brochure with **my** phone number. And people did call; believe me they called! All day, while the kids were in school the phone rang and rang. My poor wife got stuck with taking phone orders for Praying Mantis egg cases. I have to admit, the kids did have it organized. After school, one squad of kids searched the fields for egg cases, while another squad spread out over the county selling the things. This went on for several weeks with the phone ringing off the wall everyday.

My wife and I were beginning to wish that we had never set eyes on a Praying Mantis, or better yet, had never even heard of the things. Finally, the orders began to fall off. The kids never ran out of Mantis egg cases, they simply ran out of customers. I think they must have contacted every home in our county, and sold to at least half of them, if our incoming phone calls were any indication. Our son and his friends had earned a small bundle for their efforts and were quite happy with only several bags full of Mantis egg cases left over. At last, calm descended on our house and my wife and I thought we had finally seen the end of the Praying Mantis. Little did we know.

Winter came with its snow and cold winds, and we forgot all about Praying Mantises. We kept busy splitting wood for our stove and shoveling snow. We were also working on our third edition of the Poor Man's Catalog, along with building a number of projects in our basement shop, and having a ball. All in all, we had a pretty productive winter. Spring finally rolled around and we started having some mild warm days. One warm day in early June, I went to work as usual, admiring the beautiful spring day and wishing I had an excuse to take off work and stay home. At just about 11 AM I received a frantic phone call from my wife at home. She was almost hysterical, and said I must come home at once. Our big, double carport attached to the house was crawling with bugs! And she wasn't going to step foot outside until I got home and did something.

When I pulled the car into our driveway, I slowly backed it up to the front of our carport and parked it. Sure enough, she was right. The carport was literally crawling with bugs. On the walls, floor, and ceiling were thousands of little one-quarter-inch long Praying Mantises! They were everywhere. The floor of the carport actually looked like it was moving, there were so many. Looking out of the carport entrance window was my wife, almost in tears, she was so upset. She had both the storm door and entrance door locked tight, and hundreds of little Mantises were crawling all over the glass in the storm door. I had to go around to the front entrance of the house to get inside. Later, I got a large push broom and gently and carefully, swept thousands of little Mantises off our carport and into the yard. It took two days before they all finally disappeared into our yard, much to my wife's relief. It seems that the previous fall, our son had stored all of his leftover Mantis egg cases in an old, insulated milk box where the little Mantises had wintered just fine. Come spring, and warm days, they had hatched out in their thousands in our old milk box. Later, I often wondered what would have happened had our son brought the egg cases into the house, and stored them in a closet. I would have probably lost my wife!

## FOR THE MOUSE IN THE HOUSE!

For the kind-hearted, a humane mouse trap. Works for gophers too. Just take an old fruit or mayonnaise jar and cut a 1"-square hole in the metal lid. Next, cut a 1½" square from any sheet metal available. Two small holes are drilled or punched through the top of the metal square and the jar lid as shown. Hinge the metal square to the inside of the jar lid using two pieces of wire. Slightly bend the bottom edge of the metal square away from the lid to aid the mouse in pushing it open. You now have a one-way door which allows the little critter in, but not out. Add bait, screw lid on jar, and I bet you get a mouse! Then, put mouse in an envelope and mail to the IRS!

Follow the advice given above, then send for our low rent-a-barrel rates.

## SUPER SQUEEZE

Add a 3" piece of old broom handle to a used tube of caulking and you can squeeze an extra few feet of caulking from the tube. The plunger just won't get it all without help.

## BRER RABBIT'S TRAP

Bait is pushed under staple

If old Brer Rabbit has been nibbling away at your garden, and you would like to get rid of him without harming him, then this little box trap is just the ticket. Use only old weathered scrap lumber, as the little critter is very suspicious of new lumber. A loose-fitting door slides vertically in channels made by nailing cleats on each side of the entrance. The door is held open with a length of picture wire run through a hole in the roof. The free end of the wire is baited, and the bait pushed under a staple driven partway into the floor. When the little critter pulls the bait from under the staple, the trap door is released and drops. NOTE: The back of the trap is covered with chicken wire rather than a solid board. And should you catch Brer Skunk rather than Brer Rabbit, don't call me!

## POOR MAN'S BICYCLE WHEELBARROW

Build this little Bicycle Wheelbarrow and you can breeze along with loads of up to 300 lbs. with ease. Perfect for lawn or garden. The bicycle wheels make it easy to roll over lawns without damaging grass. The barrow features a front panel that slides up, making the dumping of loose material a snap. Plus, the complete body unhooks from the frame allowing it to be removed for hauling long lumber, logs, or even bulky tools. Angle iron is used in the frame adding strength to the 1¼" framing lumber making a rigid, lightweight cart. The bicycle wheels turn on standard bike axles bolted between the two angles located on each side of the frame. At rest, two wooden legs braced by 1" strap iron support the cart. All three sides and the bottom are made of ½" plywood joined by 1¼" X 2" cleats reinforced on the inside corners with angle iron. Separate iron strips protect and strengthen the floor. Two ½" X 1" cleats serve as guides for the sliding front panel and hold it in place. The sides are notched to fit over cross members of the frame. Eye hooks lock into screw eyes on the frame to hold the body of the cart in place.

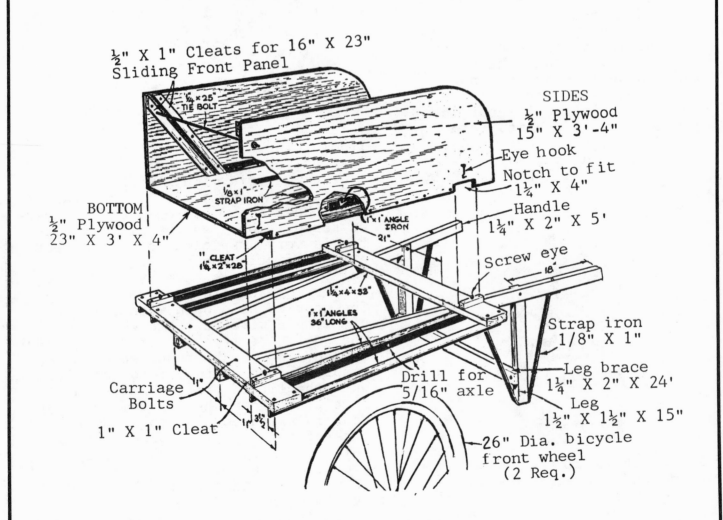

½" X 1" Cleats for 16" X 23" Sliding Front Panel

¼ x 25" TIE BOLT

⅛ x 1" STRAP IRON

1" x 1" ANGLE IRON

BOTTOM ½" Plywood 23" X 3' X 4"

" CLEAT 1¼" x 2" x 28

1¼ x 4" x 33"

1" x 1" ANGLES 36" LONG

21"

Carriage Bolts

1"

3½

1" X 1" Cleat

Drill for 5/16" axle

SIDES ½" Plywood 15" X 3'-4"

Eye hook

Notch to fit 1¼" X 4"

Handle 1¼" X 2" X 5'

Screw eye

18"

Strap iron 1/8" X 1"

Leg brace 1¼" X 2" X 24'

Leg 1½" X 1½" X 15"

26" Dia. bicycle front wheel (2 Req.)

## SLICK SNOW SHOVEL

The next time you get stuck
shoveling snow, you can make
the job a lot eaiser by applying some auto paste wax to
the inside of the snow shovel.
Rub it on and wipe it off just
as if you were polishing your
car. Wet snow will no longer
stick to your shovel and will
slide off freely.

## BARBECUE SKILLET

An old, beatup
cast-iron skillet
with holes drilled
around the outer edges
makes an excellent barbecue grill
for campers, or in an emergency.

Time is your
friend only
when used wisely.

The Poor Man

## LAZY MAN'S MOWER STARTER

Having broken the pull rope on my
recoil start power mower, I chucked
the flexible, rubber backing pad
for the disk sander into my electric
drill. Removing the recoil start
housing from the mower, I simply
pressed the pad down against the
mower starting pulley firmly, and
braced the mower with my foot. Then
I pressed the drill switch and started
the mower with little effort. This
worked so well, I never did repair
the recoil start.

All right! Who sprinkled the
Bacon Bits over their Kitty
Litter again?

# PLANTS' DELIGHT

**Window Greenhouse**

Using your original window storm-sash, you can build a mini window greenhouse that is the equal of most commercial units, at less than one-third the cost. Pick a window on the sunny side of your house and build this "Plants' Delight."

First, remove storm-sash from the window selected and chamfer the bottom. Rehang the storm-sash with two heavy-duty hinges at the top. Attach a 2" X 3" length of stock to the existing window sill using angle brackets that are slightly bent, to make the top (bottom of greenhouse) level. Cut a sheet of 3/4" exterior plywood to fit the width of your window for the flooring of your greenhouse. Attach to the length of 2" X 3" stock with wood screws. Build two triangular side sashes from 1¼" X 2" stock. Set in plain crosspieces 3/8" back from face. Nail in quarter-round molding between them to form glass rabbet. Cut triangular pieces of window glass to fit, and set in place. Fasten triangular sashes with wood screws into window storm-sash rabbet and through shelf. Protect hinged joint at the top by tacking a strip of aluminum flashing over it.

## TRIANGULAR SIDE SASH

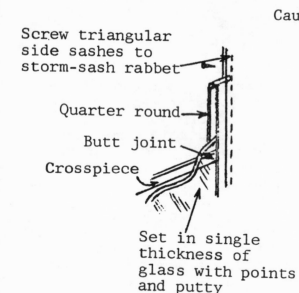

Join with long wood screws

Use flat angle bracket at 90 degree joints.

Use mending plate across joints

Hook and eyes for opening and closing positions

3/4" Exterior plywood

Caulk all exposed joints for weather seal.

Screw triangular side sashes to storm-sash rabbet

Quarter round

Butt joint

Crosspiece

Set in single thickness of glass with points and putty

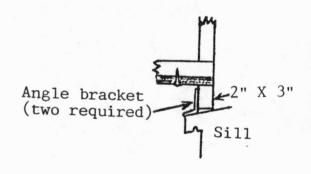

Angle bracket (two required)

2" X 3"

Sill

## DANDELION CUTTER

Got dandelions in your lawn? They are easy to get rid of with this perfect dandelion root cutter made from the handle of an old vacuum cleaner. Use a hacksaw to cut a point as shown, then sharpen sides for a cutting edge. Just stick under the dandelion and twist from side to side to cut roots.

## THE WEED WHACKER

Hacksaw blade

Screws

One or two old hacksaw blades screwed to a short broom handle or 1" dia. dowel as shown, make a wicked weed whacker. Just walk along your lawn or garden and swing the whacker with a sharp swift stroke against the base of the weed, and it's gone!

## Doodle Here!

## Help the Unfortunate! Pass this Catalog Around!

## POOR MAN'S BIRD FEEDER

Can lid is wrapped around a wood dowel.

If you will be careful and not completely cut off lids when opening cans, you can make a neat little bird feeder that will attract birds to your yard all year long.

## THE LAST COOKOUT

© 1980 VOLK

I'm not telling what I paid for it until after we've eaten it!

## SIMPLE U-BUILD GARDEN TOOLS

### POOR MAN'S HOE/WEEDER

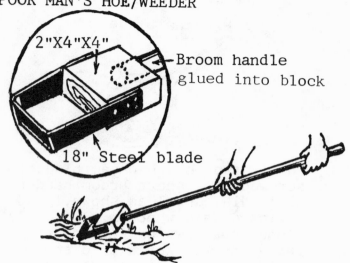

2"X4"X4"

Broom handle glued into block

18" Steel blade

I think that you will find the Poor Man's hoe/weeder handier than your regular hoe. It can be used in a chopping motion in the usual way, or it can be pulled along with the blade just under the surface to act as a shallow cultivator or weeder. The lower edge of the blade is sharpened similar to a hoe blade. It is simple to build from an old broom handle, a length of thin steel bent into a more or less "U" shape and attached to a wooden block with wood screws. This thing really eats weeds!

### AERATOR CLOGS

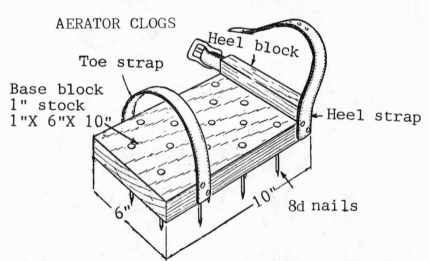

Heel block

Toe strap

Base block
1" stock
1"X 6"X 10"

Heel strap

6"

10"

8d nails

Build these simple clogs and you can aerate your lawn by simply walking around on it. The holes left in the turf allow water and fertilizer to reach root systems. And, you gotta admit, the cost is right!

### THE "CHOPPER"

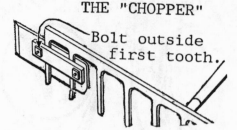

Bolt outside first tooth.

Attach an old plane or scraper blade to the end of your rake and you have a most useful weeding and cultivating tool. Also good for chopping roots. Use a flat iron strip and two bolts that will pass through the slot in the blade. Or drill bolt holes to fit.

### TRANSPLANTER TOOL

An 8" length of 1"dia. aluminum tubing cut on an easy curve to center, then along the axis for 3" gives you a narrow trowel that is perfect for lifting tiny seedlings, roots and all, from the flat.

### FORK CULTIVATOR

For you windowbox and greenhouse gardeners, an old table fork with tines bent at right angles to the handle makes an excellent rake and cultivator for use around cuttings, small plants, and seedlings.

## SUCCESS

Behind every successful man is a woman--with nothing to wear.

L.G. Glickman

## "T" BAR TRACTOR LOCK

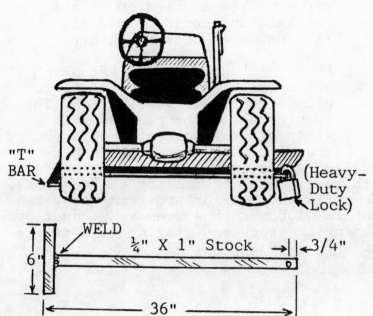

"T" BAR

(Heavy-Duty Lock)

WELD

6"

¼" X 1" Stock    →| |←3/4"

|← 36" →|

IF POLITICIANS HAD TO LIVE LIKE WORKING FOLKS WE WOULD HAVE MORE HONEST POLITICIANS.

The Poor Man

## LUBRICATING BUCKET

Having lost one good garden tractor to thieves, we devised this flat steel,"T" Bar Wheel Lock. It is simply a short 6" "T" welded across a 36" length of flat steel stock, with a hole drilled through the long end to accept the hasp of a pad-lock. This "T" bar is inserted through the wheel rims of the two rear tractor wheels. With the "T" at one end, and a heavy duty padlock at the other, it makes it almost impossible to remove the bar. The rear overhang of the tractor makes hacksawing the bar most difficult. The length of the bar should be kept as short as possible, while still allowing enough room to install the padlock. Some makes of tractors may require different lengths of bar. Use only a good quality, heavy-duty padlock. Sure beats sitting up all night with a shotgun across your lap.

To keep your garden tools clean and free of rust, just mix a little lubricating oil into a bucket of clean sand. Push the tool back and forth in the sand bucket and the sand scours off dirt and leaves a protective oil coating on the tools.

## POOR MAN'S ROOT CELLAR

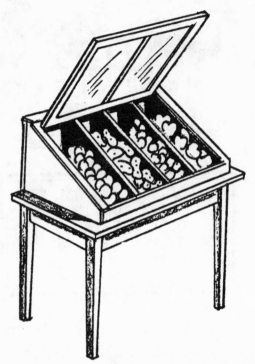

Anyone who enjoys growing their own vegetables and fruit should have a storage bin. While not actually a root cellar of old, placed in a cool, dry place this little storage bin will certainly serve the purpose. Apples, pears, plums, potatoes, onions, beets, carrots, and many other foods will stay garden-fresh when placed in this little storage bin. It is quite easily made from ¼" plywood or hardboard. The plan can be expanded to hold more storage bins than the four shown. It is designed to be mounted on a table or cabinet, and could be modified to fit inside a kitchen cabinet.

NOTE: A 1" opening is left along the bottom edge of the back panel to allow proper air ventilation. This opening should be covered with a strip of wire screen. Should you be troubled with those little pesky critters, mice, the bottom and sides of the bin should be covered with sheet metal to protect the contents. Otherwise, many families of mice will love you for providing many free meals, as ours did! A standard storm-window sash serves as a cover over the bin. Or, you can build one using 1" stock and glazing with single-strength glass.

Old storm-window sash makes an excellent cover.

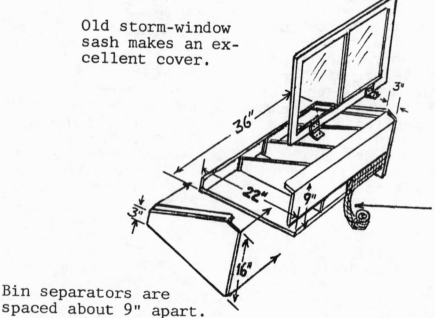

1" Air ventilation opening is covered by a strip of wire screen. If you have mice, use hardware cloth.

Bin separators are spaced about 9" apart.

## GARDENER'S KNEELING TRAY

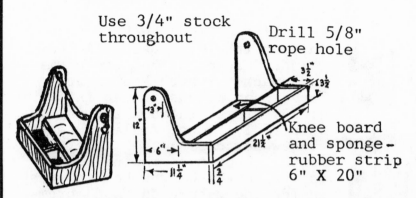

Use 3/4" stock throughout

Drill 5/8" rope hole

Knee board and sponge-rubber strip 6" X 20"

Build this little garden tray and it will make gardening a lot easier on your knees and back. Supporting yourself with your hands on the two uprights, you can kneel down on a sponge-rubber cushion built right into the garden tray. The tray is divided into two compartments, one for small garden tools, and the other for seeds, fertilizer, etc. The tray is easily carried using a short length of rope between the two uprights. After painting your favorite color, finish with a coat of Spar varnish.

FOREIGN AID SHOULD BEGIN AT HOME!

The Poor Man

## POOR MAN'S GRILL

## POOR MAN'S OUTDOOR LIGHT

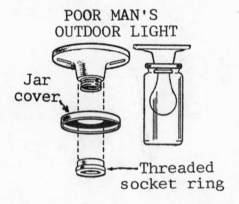

Jar cover

Threaded socket ring

Outdoor electric lights for porch, garden, or patio can be easily protected from the weather with screw-top jars with the jar lid installed between the screw-shell ring and the fixture. Just cut a hole in the lid to fit the fixture.

You can improvise a neat little barbecue grill using four empty beer or soda pop cans along with an upside-down metal garbage can lid. Put the four empty cans under each side of the lid, pour in some charcoal and place a grate on top. If you will first line the inside of your grill with sheets of aluminum foil it will reflect more heat to your grate and make cleanup much easier.

78

ALL-SEASON WINDOW BOX

This little window box is unique in that it can be used all year round. Suspended from two aluminum brackets which hook over large wood screws turned into the window frame, the box serves as a beautiful, flower-filled outdoor window box during the summer months. When the growing season is over outside, the box is swung inside and rehung on wood screws attached to the inside window frame. The box can be emptied and filled with your potted plants for window beauty during the cold months. The entire box is made from 3/4" stock and is lined with heavy-duty aluminum foil on the inside when complete. The aluminum foil will help to protect the wooden box for long life. Just remember to poke drain holes in the foil over the drain holes in the bottom of the box. When the box is inside the house, the drain holes can be covered with a folded sheet of aluminum foil along the bottom of the box to protect your floor from drainage. Paint the box to match your home's trim and finish with a heavy coat of Spar varnish.

Those with artistic talents might like to decorate the front of the window box with their own paintings or with decals.

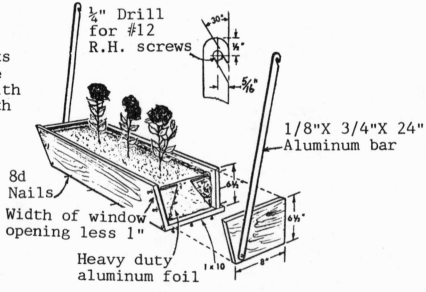

¼" Drill for #12 R.H. screws

1/8"X 3/4"X 24" Aluminum bar

8d Nails

Width of window opening less 1"

Heavy duty aluminum foil

Four evenly spaced ½" drain holes are drilled across the bottom of box.

## PERMANENT GARDEN SEAT

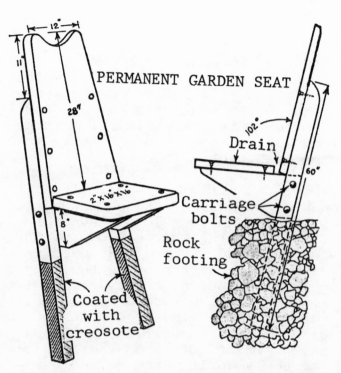

Drain

Carriage bolts

Rock footing

Coated with creosote

Rather than pay fancy prices for that light aluminum lawn furniture, you might consider building simple, permanent, lawn and garden seats from wood that will last a while. Creosote all parts that go underground, keep all above-ground parts well painted, and you will have furniture that will last for years. The 60° tilt allows water to drain naturally.

## POOR MAN'S SPREADER MARKER

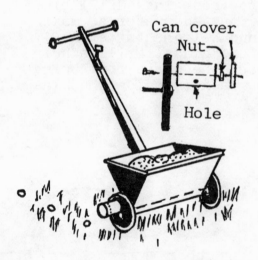

Can cover

Nut

Hole

Make this simple lime-holding marker for your lawn spreader and you will no longer have any overlapping problem when applying fertilizer or weed killer to your lawn. The marker is a baking-powder can with a small hole drilled through one side. Attached to the wheel, it deposits a spot of lime on each turn of the spreader wheel. The resulting row of white dots serves as a guide in lining up the hopper for the next pass.

## DOWNSPOUT SPLASH RIM

An old tire rim can prevent downspout runoff from washing away your lawn. Sink the tire rim flush with the ground and fill it with coarse gravel.

## MINI TERRARIUM

Mount a 10¢ store spherical fish bowl
to an upside-down, discarded salad bowl,
fill with filtered compost mixed with
sand, a few small plants, and you have
your own Mini Terrarium. The large
opening in the top of the bowl makes
the plants easy to care for.

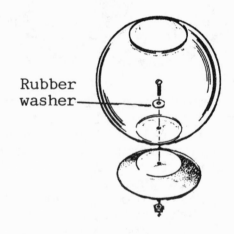

The Mini Terrarium is quite easy to
make, and most of the parts can be
purchased in your local 10¢ store. (Is
there anything that can be purchased
for only 10¢ anymore?) We used an old,
discarded, plastic salad bowl for our
base, but you can turn your own from
wood if you wish. Use a small brass tube
(about 1/8") with the cutting edge serrated
with a file, to drill a small hole in the
exact center bottom of the fish bowl. (Or
use the soldring iron method described on
page 32.) Chuck the brass tube into your
electric drill or drill press, and slowly feed
carborundum dust or fine sand to your improvised glass drill bit.
Pout the abrasive under the bit as needed, and add water to make
a thick paste. Use a slow spindle speed, and a light but steady
pressure while feeding the cutting bit to the glass. Drill a hole
in the exact center of your base, and attach the glass bowl using
a 1-inch nut and bolt, along with a rubber washer inside the glass
bowl. Use a metal washer under the base.

Feed the abrasive to the
cutting bit using a folded
bit of paper. Add water to
make a paste.

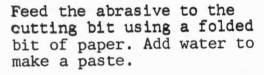

Rubber
washer

## POOR BIRD'S HOUSE

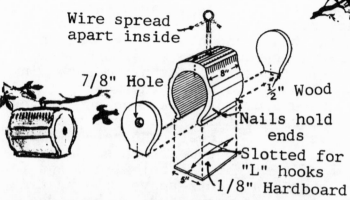

Wire spread apart inside

7/8" Hole

½" Wood

Nails hold ends

Slotted for "L" hooks

1/8" Hardboard

An old auto-tire casing can make a neat, weatherproof birdhouse. In fact, it can make five or six of them. Just scrollsaw the wooden ends to fit flush inside the ends of the casing, then nail in place. The bottom is just scrap wood slotted at the ends so that it can be held in place with an L-hook driven into each end piece. Makes for easy cleaning. The entrance hole shown is sized for the tiny wren but can be larger for your favorite birds.

## SOCK IT TO UM!

Take a pair of old, heavy, cotton socks and slip over the upper ends of your ladder to keep from marring the siding. Fold to the front so that ladder rests on double thickness of socks.

## POOR BIRD'S NESTING SHELF

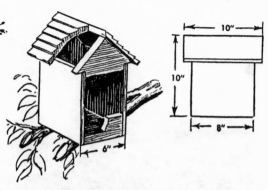

## BUTT HINGE WINDOW LOCK

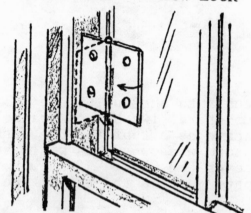

Mount a butt hinge on the upper window sash as shown and you have a simple window lock by swinging the hinge leaf out 90°. Makes a perfect lock for garden sheds, basement windows, and workshops.

### HOMEOWNER'S LAW

Your neighbor borrowed the exact tool that you need, but he moved away last week!

YOU KNOW  YOU CAN'T WIN!

### HOMEOWNER'S 2nd LAW

You managed to borrow the exact tool that you needed, then broke it!

## PORTABLE HOTHOUSE

This little wooden cabinet-type hothouse was built by my father over twenty-five years ago. It works just as well now as it did when brand new. Being small and compact, it can be moved around at will. A single 100-watt lightbulb mounted in line with an old house thermostat (available used from most wrecking and salvage companies) maintains a uniform temperature at very low cost. The hothouse is divided into two compartments. One for the heating lightbulb below, and one for the young new plants above. The heating compartment is insulated on the sides and bottom with any good-grade insulating board. We lined the plant compartment with asphalt roofing paper (tar paper) which extends out through a slot cut into one end of the cabinet. This allows for the escape of excess moisture. Two hinged frames which are glazed with standard window glass serve as a roof for the hothouse and admit sunlight. A pair of old storm window sashes would serve just as well. 3/4" stock was used to cover the 2" X 4" framework of the cabinet. Note the use of roofing paper across the top of the cabinet to help seal the window frames.

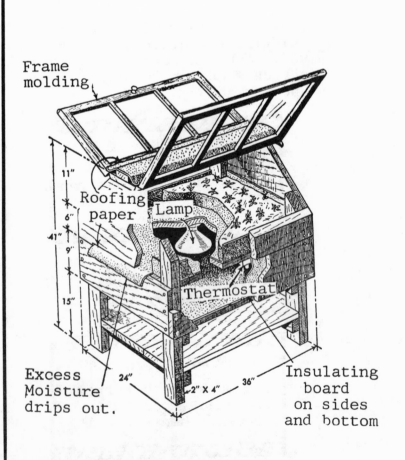

Frame molding

11"
Roofing paper
Lamp
6"
41"
9"
Thermostat
15"

Excess Moisture drips out.
24"
2" X 4"
36"
Insulating board on sides and bottom

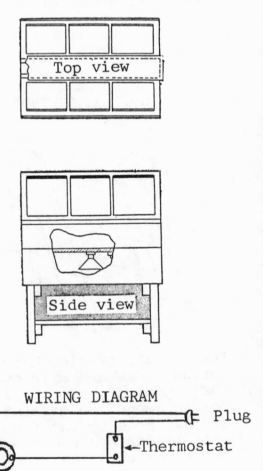

Top view

Side view

WIRING DIAGRAM

Plug
Thermostat
Lamp

## POOR MAN'S GREAT GARDEN WAR

Having a fair-sized backyard, we decided that a small vegetable garden would be both fun and money-saving. Little did we know. After buying the seeds, fertilizer, and assorted garden tools, I started to wonder just how much money we would save. But, like all good gardeners, I just visualized those beautiful red tomatoes, golden sweet corn, and delicious green beans just flowing out of the garden and onto our table. Unfortunately, some other little critters were having the same ideas. It was almost as if I rang the dinner bell as I dropped seeds into the ground. And those seeds must have made a terrible racket as they hit the ground, because they woke up every bug for miles around.

As soon as little green shoots started to poke out of the ground, I was in there with my trusty hoe, looking for weeds. Somehow I wiped out two rows of beans before discovering they weren't weeds. Well, live and learn, I thought. And I did. Almost as soon as the little green plants started to develop leaves, something was right there to welcome them. With open mouths! It got so bad that my plants looked like rows and rows of little green sticks. This is war, I told myself as I started spraying bug juice all over the garden. And I was right. It was a war, and I was on the losing end. They had an army march in at night and nibble away, then the day army marched in and took over munching at dawn. It seemed that the more bug spray I poured over the plants, the more bugs came to dinner. Not only that, but I strongly suspect that bug spray is really weed fertilizer. Weeds were popping up everywhere. They seemed to grow a foot higher over night. Bugs were using them to pole vault onto my plants! Something had to be done; things were getting out of hand. Thinking craftily, I decided to outmaneuver the bugs. I would allow the weeds to grow, and they would camouflage my vegetables. When the weeds got thick enough, the bugs wouldn't be able to find my tender plants. Wrong again! The bugs used the weeds to hide from the bug spray, then attacked when I was gone. By now I had the healthiest looking weeds, and worst looking vegetables in the county. My weeds easily could have walked away with first place at the county fair.

84

Then one bright morning when I went down to the garden to hoe out the weeds, it happened! As I was laying into the weeds with my trusty hoe, I heard a strange rustling. Suddenly something shot out of the weeds right between my feet, bowling me over. The bugs had finally done it--brought out their reinforcements--an attack rabbit trained in guerrilla warfare! He was sleek, fast, and cunning. And as mean as they come. As he shot out of my garden patch, I swear he stopped, raised up on his hind legs, and gave me the clenched-fist salute. I knew then that he would be back again. So I laid my plans accordingly. No rabbit was going to run me out of my own garden, even if he was attack trained. So, the next morning I got up very early and loaded my heavy artillery. Sneaking down to my garden under cover of early dawn, I lay in ambush for that crazy rabbit. Sure enough, by listening carefully I could hear him sneaking around in the weeds--probably laying his own ambush for me. But this time I was ready for him. No more Mr. Nice Guy. I was going to let him have it. When I saw the weed tops tremble with his passing, I quick, pumped six fast twelve-gauge rounds filled with birdshot into the area. Never touched the rabbit, but sure did clean out my weed patch garden! Have you ever seen ripe tomatoes hit with six rounds of birdshot? Nothing like it! Instant tomato juice. And the rabbit? He was last seen advancing to the rear at a fast hop. Probably back home by now, telling all his buddies war stories about the Great Garden War.

THE POOR MAN

# Photography

The photographic projects shown below are not available
in <u>this</u> catalog. They are available in our self-published
Poor Man's Catalog #5.

Eat your hearts out fellows!

Ha! And when his
wife catches him
she'll cut his out!

86

## THE SUPER-COMPUTERIZED AUTOMATIC
## IBM SLR 35mm CAMERA

Dear Friends, I would be the first to admit that I know very little about cameras. I have been known to have trouble finding the "push" button. Once, I took a whole roll of film with the lens cap still on. So when my good wife got on me about buying one of those new-fangled, super-computerized, automatic-sanitized, idiot-proof, SLR 35mm cameras, I did have my doubts. But she had seen them advertised on the television, and assured me how easy they were to operate.

So, when her thirty-ninth birthday rolled around again, I rambled on down to the local camera store. I asked the clerk to show me some of those fancy 35mm cameras like's advertised on the TV.  I said "Lay them on me, boy!"  And he did.  He piled a whole bunch of those pretty little cameras right up on the counter. I picked out a fancy-looking one from the top of the pile and started fiddling around with all the little buttons, switches, and knobs, just like I knew what I was doing. I looked her over real careful like, then gave her a few sharp raps on the counter top. I held it up to my ear and shook it, and darned if I couldn't hear little things rattling around in there. I looked the clerk right in the eye (noticing that he seemed a little green around the gills) and said, "You know, they don't build them like they used to." He had to agree, as he opened the back door of the thing and all those little springs and such fell out.

While he was putting all the little parts into a pile, I reached around behind the counter and picked up one of those telescope things. The kind that screw into the front of a camera. I put it up to my eye but couldn't see a blame thing. I twisted around the rings on the thing but nothing seemed to work. No matter how I tried to focus it, it just wouldn't work. Finally, just as I was getting ready to give her a few whacks on the countertop, the clerk reached over sort of shaky-like, and removed the telescope from my hand. By now I was sure I had him convinced that I knew just what I was about when it came to cameras. I could tell, because he was sweating a lot. He gave me a sickly grin as he quickly started putting all the cameras back behind the counter. Then he looked up and said, "Sir, I can see that you know your cameras." I had him! So when he reached down behind the counter again I knew he was going to come up with one of the really good cameras. The ones they kept for special customers who knew their stuff.

Sure enough, he laid a real pretty little thing up on the counter and started telling me all about it. Talking real fast and watching that camera in my hands like he thought I might drop it or something. It was special all right--a computerized automatic! He said that all you had to do was point the thing in the right direction and the camera would do the rest. He said it was almost idiot-proof and would be a perfect camera for me. Little did he know that I was getting it for my wife, who doesn't know anything about cameras. Then he started telling me about all the accessories and attachments that could be used with the camera--things like telephoto lenses, wide-angle lenses, filters, flash units, and all sorts of good camera stuff. I was beginning to suspect that these camera people had been taking lessons from the Detroit car people. These little cameras have more add-ons and accessories than a new Detroit car. Why, any minute I was expecting him to mention power steering, and maybe a new flush toilet attached to the rear.

Then he leaned over the counter and whispered that this was the only camera made that the rich folks use--said they save 'em special just for doctors, dentists, and rich Arab oil sheiks. Well, now he had my ear, but it was what he said next that really sold me. He leaned a little closer over the counter and said in a low whisper "it's imported" and gave me a wink. "Besides that, it's IBM." That did it for me. Everybody knows that you never sell your stock in IBM (I had heard that once in a song). So I said, "How much?" Now, I gotta admit, the price sorta staggered me. And when I got back up off the floor, I told him flat out that while I wanted only the best, I wasn't figuring on putting a second mortgage on the house to get it. I told him that before I paid that price, they would have to put four wheels and a steering wheel on the thing. Finally, after a lot of dickering around we settled on a price. When I got it back home, I opened up the package and sure enough, that clerk was right. It was an IBM import. Stamped right in the case was ITTY BITTY MACHINE WORKS, HONG KONG.

## COLOR PRINT PAINTING

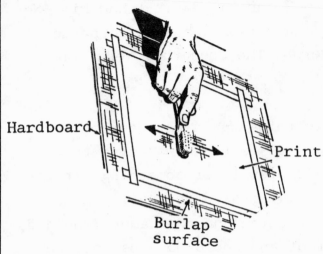

Hardboard

Print

Burlap surface

You can give a color print the texture of an oil painting by simply taping the print face down on a piece of hardboard covered with burlap cloth. Stretch the burlap tightly under the hardboard. Tape print, then rub the rounded back of a toothbrush over the surface of the print embossing the texture of the burlap on the print.

## FLOODLIGHT COOLER

You can lengthen the life of the bulb, prevent damage to the socket, and make it much cooler for your subject, by simply drilling a series of small ¼" holes around the base of the flood reflector allowing built up heat to escape.

## DEVELOPING AID

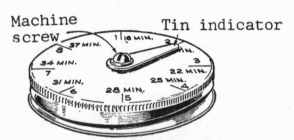

Machine screw

Tin indicator

An old jar lid marked as shown, with a tin indicating hand mounted in the center shows at a glance the developing time required for each successive batch of film. And it keeps track of the number of times the film developer has been used.

If that clown says "Ring Around the Collar" one more time I'm gonna punch his lights out!

# MINI PORTABLE DARK ROOM

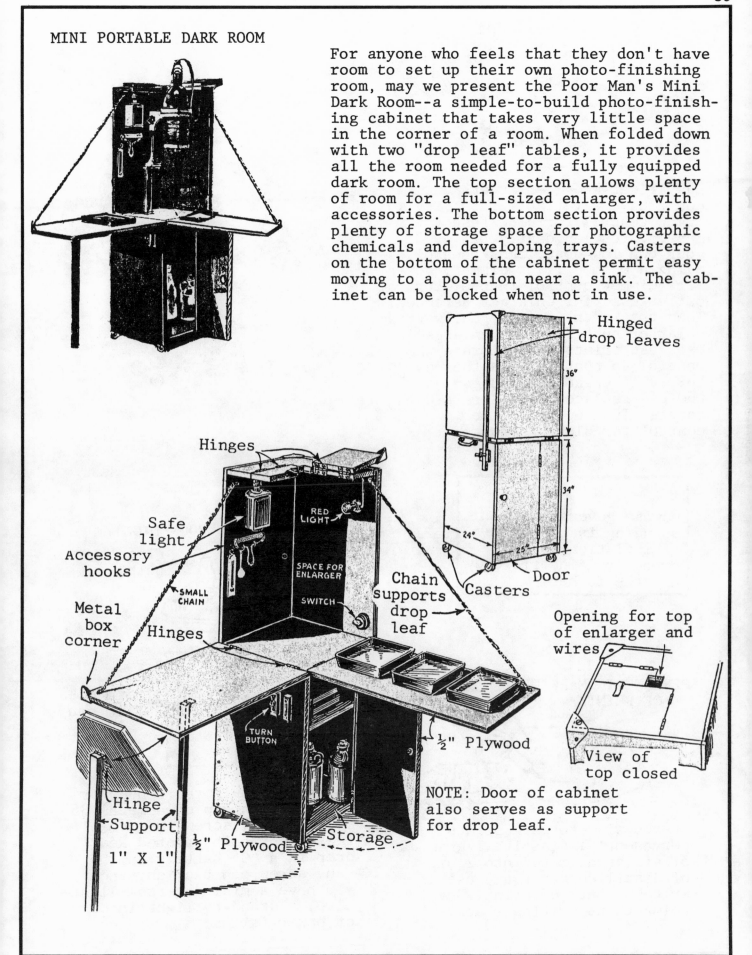

For anyone who feels that they don't have room to set up their own photo-finishing room, may we present the Poor Man's Mini Dark Room--a simple-to-build photo-finishing cabinet that takes very little space in the corner of a room. When folded down with two "drop leaf" tables, it provides all the room needed for a fully equipped dark room. The top section allows plenty of room for a full-sized enlarger, with accessories. The bottom section provides plenty of storage space for photographic chemicals and developing trays. Casters on the bottom of the cabinet permit easy moving to a position near a sink. The cabinet can be locked when not in use.

Hinged drop leaves

36"

34"

24"

25"

Door

Casters

Hinges

Safe light

Accessory hooks

SMALL CHAIN

RED LIGHT

SPACE FOR ENLARGER

SWITCH

Chain supports drop leaf

Metal box corner

Hinges

TURN BUTTON

½" Plywood

Opening for top of enlarger and wires

View of top closed

Hinge

Support

1" X 1"

½" Plywood

Storage

NOTE: Door of cabinet also serves as support for drop leaf.

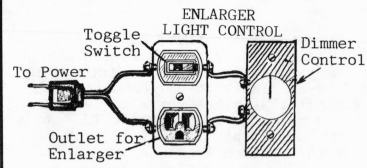

ENLARGER
LIGHT CONTROL

Toggle
Switch

Dimmer
Control

To Power

Outlet for
Enlarger

Many older-model enlargers
don't have a variable intensity
light control for slow-fast
papers. You can easily build
your own low-cost light control
using a common light dimmer.
Wire dimmer control into electrical
outlet used for enlarger as shown.
Then obtain the next higher wattage
enlarger bulb for your enlarger.
Use test prints to calibrate the
control so that it dims the new
bulb to the same brightness as
the old replaced bulb for fast
papers. Turn up the dimmer
control for slow papers.

Do It
Yourself
and SAVE!

INFLATION

Unwise government over-
spending is the mother
of inflation. Waste,
greed, and inefficiency
are the father.

MINI DARKROOM LIGHT

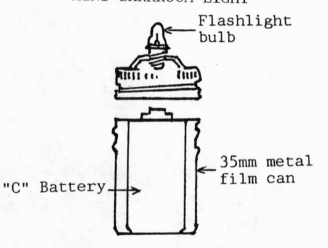

Flashlight
bulb

35mm metal
film can

"C" Battery

PERMANENT MARKING
OF PRINTS

If you wish to mark prints
permanently, dissolve 1 gram
of silver nitrate into 2 oz.
of distilled water and use to
write on back of print. Developing turns writing black.

Punch a hole in the center of
the screw-on cap of a metal 35
mm film can, screw in a small
flashlight bulb painted Red,
drop in a "C" battery in the
can, screw cap back on, and
you have a mini darkroom light--
also, a stand-by light in case
of power failure.

# POOR MAN'S MINI-TRIPOD

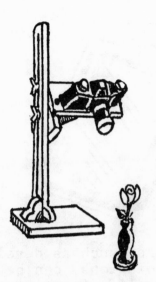

For the photographer who takes close-ups or any other type of table-top photography, our little Mini Tripod makes an excellent camera support. It is completely adjustable for both height and angle. By shifting the camera and tripod alternately, you can get practically a universal adjustment.

The Mini Tripod is quite simple to build. You can use plywood as shown, or use any solid hardwood. The cost is practically nothing if you use shop scraps. While the drawing shows all of the detail for building the tripod, you should note the half-circle quadrant which is laid out in 15° angles. Holes are drilled at these angle points allowing small bolts and wing nuts to shift and lock the camera at any desired angle. The camera support is screwed to the straight edge of the quadrant and is reinforced by an off-center brace. This is located to permit easy access to the center bolt. A ¼" stove bolt of the proper length for your camera usually fits the threaded tripod bushing of most American-made cameras. Foreign-made cameras usually require a special bushing. Your local camera store should be able to provide you with a metric-sized bolt with enough length to fit through the camera support and fit your camera's bushing. Just drill the proper size hole in the camera support and insert the tripod screw and you are ready for business.

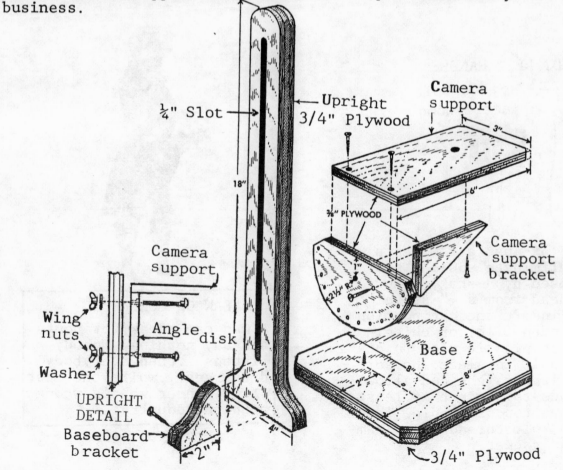

## MEASURE METER

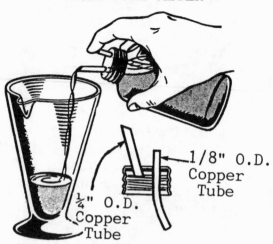

1/8" O.D. Copper Tube

¼" O.D. Copper Tube

Build this simple little pouring cap and you can measure out liquids to the drop. Finger pressure over the smaller tube controls air intake. Just drill two holes in the metal screw cap, insert two short lengths of tubing, and bend as shown. Allows precision pouring of liquid photo chemicals.

## CLEANER KEEPER

Tray solutions, such as developing and fixing solutions, can be given a much longer life if protected from evaporation, dust, and oxidation. A simple method of doing this is to cut a piece of polyethylene sheeting to the size of the surface and float it on top of the solution in the tray. Take care to always use the same sheeting for the same solution.

## STEADY REST HANDLE

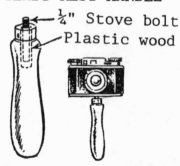

¼" Stove bolt
Plastic wood

At a cost of just a few cents you can eliminate spoiled pictures caused by a shaky camera. Cut the head from a ¼" stove bolt and insert the cut portion into a wooden file, or chisel handle. Use plastic wood to anchor the bolt in place. Be sure the bolt is straight and allow the threads to project at least 3/16" above top of handle. Then just turn bolt threads into camera tripod socket.

### LAW OF CONGRESS
A man can speak for hours and say nothing. Nobody listens...then everybody disagrees...while the rest of us wonder what's wrong with the country!

POOR MAN'S DARKROOM EASEL

Could you use a good darkroom easel that is specially designed for making borderless enlargements? Look no further, my friend. Using an 11" X 16" piece of scrap 3/4" plywood, an 11" X 15" sheet of 3/16" glass, a piece of felt, two butt hinges, some wood scraps, and two hours of your time, you have a darkroom easel as good as any expensive professional model. The large size of this easel makes it indispensable for making printing paper negatives and prints. And for enlarging, it can't be beat.

If you have access to a drill press, drilling holes in the glass is easy. Make a mound of putty around the area to be drilled and mix a paste of carborundum and water. Put paste inside putty mound and gently press a thin-walled steel tube (used as drill) into the paste with drill press running at slow speed. Or see page 32 of this book for another method.

Drill two 3/32" holes in glass.

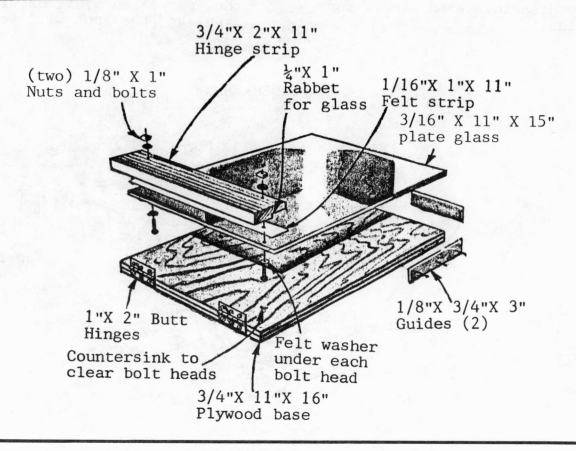

3/4"X 2"X 11"
Hinge strip

(two) 1/8" X 1"
Nuts and bolts

¼"X 1"
Rabbet
for glass

1/16"X 1"X 11"
Felt strip

3/16" X 11" X 15"
plate glass

1"X 2" Butt
Hinges

Countersink to
clear bolt heads

Felt washer
under each
bolt head

3/4"X 11"X 16"
Plywood base

1/8"X 3/4"X 3"
Guides (2)

## STEREO PICTURES WITH YOUR 35-MM CAMERA

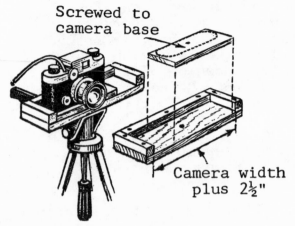

Screwed to camera base

Camera width plus 2½"

You can make pictures for stereoscopic viewing using your 35-MM camera. Build this simple little wooden slide box as shown to fit your camera. NOTE: The holder must be 2½" wider than your camera. First, a picture is snapped with the camera on the right side of the holder. Then the camera is shifted to the left side and a second picture is taken of the same subject. Of course, the subject must not move. Pairs of pictures can then be mounted in stereo slides for viewing.

## PRINT FLATTENER

You can flatten a curled print by placing it emulsion side down in a large heavy book. Grasp the edge of the print, and pull it out of the book at a sharp upward angle while exerting light pressure on the book binding. Repeat several times, reversing print edge for a full flat surface.

## SPOTS BE-GONE

Black spots on a print caused by pinholes in the negative can be removed by applying a tiny bit of tincture of iodine to the spot. Then a bit of plain hypo, and the spot will be gone.

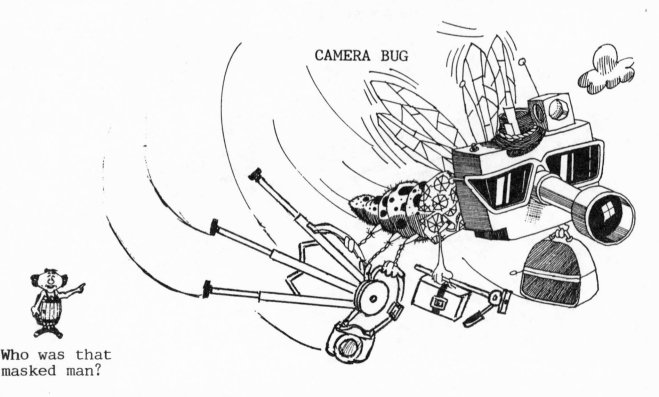

CAMERA BUG

Who was that masked man?

## POOR MAN'S SPOT

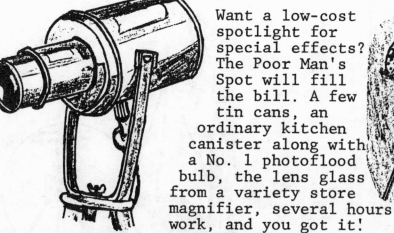

Want a low-cost spotlight for special effects? The Poor Man's Spot will fill the bill. A few tin cans, an ordinary kitchen canister along with a No. 1 photoflood bulb, the lens glass from a variety store magnifier, several hours work, and you got it!

Take a 5" X 7" kitchen canister and center a lamp receptacle inside the bottom center. Pierce mounting holes, and drill or punch ventilation and electric cord holes in canister as shown. Remove the bottom from a ½-pint paint can, and cut the top flange from a similar paint can. Cut a hole the size of the flange opening in the center of the canister cover.

Holding cover, flange, and canister in sequence, drill holes for the four 1/8" X 3/4" bolts that hold them together. Take a standard, 2-5/8" soup can with top already removed, and cut a hole 1/8" smaller than your magnifier lens diameter in the bottom. Form a lens-retaining ring from stiff wire, and install lens.

Cement a felt strip around soup can to make a snug, sliding fit inside the paint can. Wire the lamp receptacle taking care to line the electrical cord entry hole (into canister) with rubber or plastic grommet to prevent cutting wires. Wire an ON-OFF switch outside the canister.

Build the spotlight holder from 1/8" X 1" X 20" strap-iron, bending inside slightly 3" from bottom as shown. Drill ¼" holes in bottom of strap and in the two sides to attach to canister.

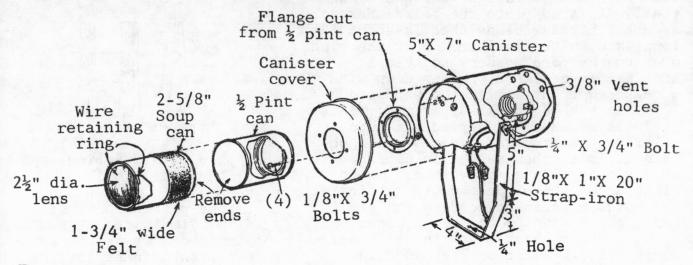

Four bolts secure the middle can to the canister and flange.

## PRECISION PAPER CUTTER

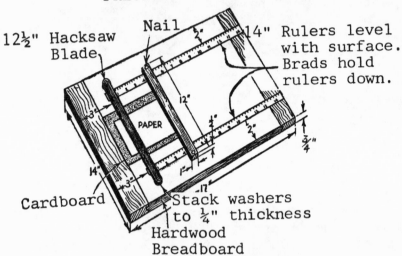

12½" Hacksaw Blade · Nail · 14" Rulers level with surface. Brads hold rulers down. · PAPER · Cardboard · Stack washers to ¼" thickness · Hardwood Breadboard

We originally built this little paper cutter to cut note pads from scrap paper. Then my son found it so handy for cutting negatives and photographic papers that we decided to show it here. Using a piece of hardwood 14" wide by 17" long, you first make two grooves in the board to accept two wooden rulers 14" long. The rulers must be inserted into grooves and nailed into position. They must fit flat and even with the surface of the board--actually "inlayed" into the board. Next, secure a hacksaw blade that is about 12½" long, and quite flexible. Mount the blade over two or more washers so that it stands ¼" over board. Fasten down with ½" wood screws. Cut a piece of wood stock 12" long, by ½" thick, by 1" wide. This strip is moved along surface of both rulers until required paper size is obtained. It is then tacked into place. To use, simply slip as many sheets as possible under the blade, and tap against the movable strip of wood. With left hand, press down on blade and paper while using a sharp razor blade to cut paper along straight edge of hacksaw blade. Always use cardboard under paper.

## EMERGENCY TRIPOD

Camera · Tin can

Just three fairly straight sticks inserted into a tin can as shown give you an emergency tripod. Just remember that the camera is not secured and must be held to prevent it from falling.

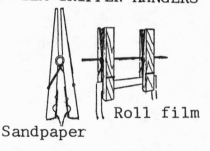

## FILM GRIPPER HANGERS

Sandpaper · Roll film

A pair of old spring-type clothespins provide a secure grip on wet and slippery sheet or roll film. Simply cement small strips of wet or dry sandpaper onto inner jaws of clothespins.

# LIGHTING TIPS

Rather than screwing a reflector photoflood directly into a ceiling fixture for overhead lighting, fit the photoflood with a swivel joint by simply turning two double sockets into it. This allows the light to be focused at a variety of angles to any part of the room.

## TAPE MEASURE LAMP CORD

Wrap white strips of tape around flood reflector electric cord at one foot intervals and you have a made-to-order tape measure for positioning lamps at the proper distances from subjects.

## LAMP CLAMP

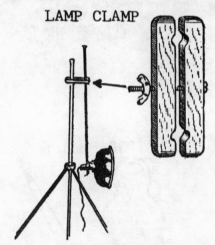

Trying to position a photoflood mounted on a light stand near the floor for desired lighting effects can be a problem. Build this novel little wood clamp from two pieces of hardwood that have been notched near both ends to clamp over light-stand shaft and drilled for a bolt and wing nut, and you have a useful lamp clamp.

## LE HOT ONE

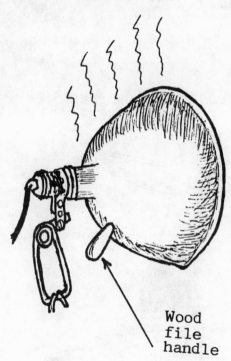

Wood file handle

You can prevent burned fingers when adjusting a flood reflector bowl by installing a wood file handle with a screw. Makes a convenient handle.

## RAIL SCALE

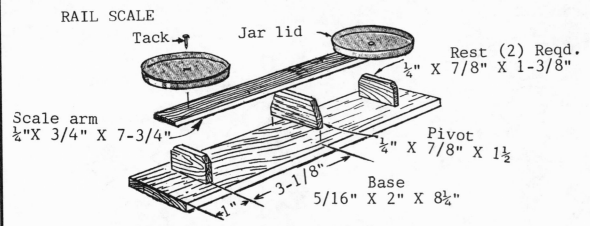

Tack →

Jar lid

Rest (2) Reqd.
¼" X 7/8" X 1-3/8"

Scale arm
¼"X 3/4" X 7-3/4"

Pivot
¼" X 7/8" X 1½

3-1/8"

1"

Base
5/16" X 2" X 8¼"

This handy little darkroom scale
can be built from scraps for just
a few cents. Yet it can weigh out
photo chemicals just as easily as
an expensive commercial model. Just
be sure to balance the scale arm
carefully before final assembly.

POLITICIAN AT WORK

## POOR PHOTOGRAPHER'S TANK ROCKER

Wood rocker

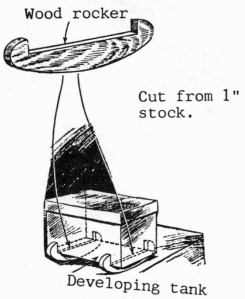

Cut from 1"
stock.

Developing tank

Cut snugly to fit your developing
tank, a pair of these wooden rockers will gently keep your tank
rocking during development period.

## PHOTOGRAPH INK

Plain old liquid white
shoe polish makes an ideal
ink for writing on the
dark areas of photographs.
Use a regular pen point
available at most stationery stores. It also works
fine on blueprints.

STOVEPIPE FILM DRIER

You can build a very efficient, low-cost film drier for your darkroom using just stovepipe, coathanger wire, scrap lumber, an electric light socket, and a few wooden clothespins. Not only does this simple drier increase drying speed and give negatives of finer grain, but it also protects drying film from airborne dust. It is quite simple to build and use, and will dry up to four rolls of film at one time.

Build each cross-base piece at least 24" long, making sure that base sits level when complete. Then install electric light socket with 60-watt bulb.

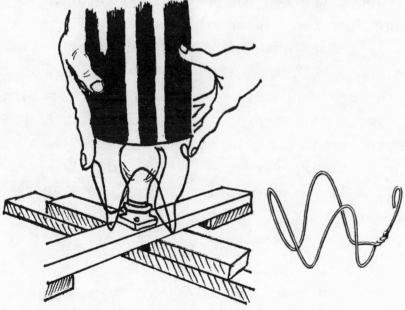

To prevent film from curling while drying, a clothespon is attached to the bottom of each film as a weight.

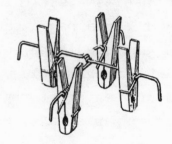

The film rack is made from coathanger wire bent as shown.

The spring clip which holds the stovepipe on wood base is bent from coathanger wire.

## BATTUB TEA

No, it's not the same as bathtub gin. You don't have to drink this stuff. It would probably curl your eyebrows and rust your pipes! Bathtub tea is the Poor Man's version of a special hot, herb bath that my wife had read an article about. I only use it on special occasions, like at wood splitting time. I had been out in our back yard splitting wood for our stove, when I caught a bad case of the wood splitter's flu. This is the flu that settles right in the small of your back, after you've been fighting a thirteen-pound sledge hammer. And the hammer wins! Either I'm getting older (no chance, I'm holding at 39!), or that hammer is putting on weight. It's been winning a lot lately. So, I'm standing there holding my aching back when my wife calls with something like "Come on in, have I got a bath for you!" or words to that effect. Sure enough, when I stumbled inside she had a tub full of steaming hot water waiting for me. She had already made our herbal tea bag which is really a wash cloth filled with some special herbs, then folded to form a bag with the end tightly closed by twisting a rubber band around it. She dropped the tea bag wash cloth into the steaming water while I got ready. The tea bag should seep in the hot water for about ten minutes to allow the release of the soothing herb oils. Then I jumped in. Oh Wow! Talk about relaxing. Those little herbs just seem to work magic by jumping through your skin and comforting those aching muscles--best thing in the world for wood splitter's flu. You just give the tea bag a squeeze every once in a while to release more herb oils and use it to scrub yourself, making sure you go over all those tired aching muscles. Nothing like it. If you would like to try your own bathtub tea, just try the following recipe. Mix together about one cup of: two parts sage, with one part each of comfrey leaf, mugwort, German chamomile, and white oak bark. Dump into a clean wash cloth and drop into a steaming hot tub. Then enjoy! You should be able to find most of the herbs required at your local health food store or plant nursery. They are also available thru the mail from herb growers. Don't forget your rubber duck!

# Sports

The sports projects shown below are not available in <u>this</u> catalog. They are available in our self-published Poor Man's Catalog #5.

J.BLACKWELL

Quick! Paint the cows blue, he's going hunting!

## POOR MAN'S FISH STORY

I have just two sports that I am really interested in. Luckily, they both require just about the same equipment, which makes it a little easier on the pocketbook. But what makes my sport really interesting is that if I time it just right, I can play both at the same time. Now, some folks might think that it's just a little unusual to try and play two sports at the same time. How can you give full time and attention to two different sports? And the answer is that it's not easy. It does take a great deal of extra effort and heavy concentration. I suppose you could say that I try harder. Sometimes it just wears me out, and I go home beat. But I can always spring back, ready for action the next day, I always make sure that my equipment is fully operational and ready to go. My reel is oiled, my sun shades are polished, my casting rod is free of tangles, and my binoculars are strapped around my neck. Sometimes, I even stop and buy bait. Then I am ready to enjoy my two sports--fishing and girl watching (not necessarily in that order). I have found that the sunniest part of the day is usually the best time for surf fishing. Few fish are biting and lots of sweet young things are wiggling about on the beach. Almost makes it worth getting sunburned! Of course, once in a while some stupid fish will bite and spoil everything. I learned the hard way. Once I was giving full time and attention to this young thing walking by, when this crazy fish grabbed my bait. He kept jerking on the line, wouldn't give up, and finally, broke my line of concentration. This fish had no class at all. He demanded attention by jumping out of the water, splashing around, and making a general nuisance of himself. Finally, in desperation, I grabbed my trusty fishing knife and cut the line. But it was too late. The sweet young thing was gone. Then to make matters worse, that ungrateful fish swam right up between my feet and I had no choice but to take it home and clean the thing. Ruined my entire day! The moral to this story is just this: Never, never, bait your hook when you're doing something really important, like girl watching, or the good one's are likely to wiggle away!

## FISHING ROD RACK

A few old wooden clothespins with heads removed are cemented in ½" holes drilled into a length of 1" X 2" scrap wood stock. Stain and varnish, and you have a neat, low-cost fishing rod rack that can be mounted on any wall or even inside a closet on the back of the door.

## FLYING DUCKS ORNAMENT OR WALL PLAQUE

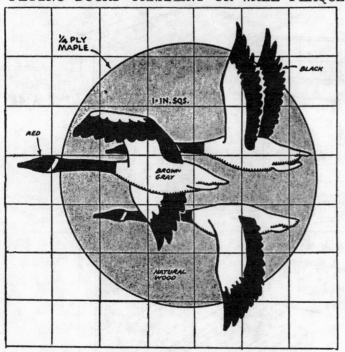

¼ PLY MAPLE

BLACK

1 IN. SQS.

RED

BROWN GRAY

NATURAL WOOD

Cut from ¼" plywood and paint as marked. Used as ornament on gun cabinet door shown elsewhere in this section. Can also be used as wall plaque. To enlarge ducks, lay out graph on paper using 1" or larger squares.

## FOR THE NIGHT FISHERMAN

Notched Line Holder

Gap

Thin Spring Steel

Copper Wire Through Stick

The night fisherman should enjoy this simple night fishing rig. When a fish bites, pulling the line, a contact is made, lighting a small flashlight bulb. The fishing pole is simply a length of wood to which a strip of spring steel is screwed to hold the line. A small L-shaped bracket holds the bulb and is in constant contact with the center terminal of a flashlight battery and the spring steel. The battery is held on the pole with a sheet-metal strap. A copper wire passes through the wood pole and contacts the bottom of the battery. The copper wire is attached to a metal strip on the opposite side of the pole which forms the gapper, or contact. The gap should be about ½".

## ECONOMY GUN CABINET

Flying duck door ornament details shown elsewhere in this section.

In need of a gun cabinet, I spent considerable time looking around local stores for one that would fit both my needs and pocketbook. I found a number that would fit my needs, but none that would fit my pocketbook. I had one salesman tell me that the reason his gun cabinets were so high is because they were made from real wood! I shudder to think what the others were made of. Needless to say, I built my own hammer-and-nail job--a plywood and pine cabinet, with the door housed between the sides and stopped by rabbeted ledges on top and bottom. A moulded butt pit which can be cut by using a moulding head with table tilted 6°. Make successive cuts, resetting the depth each time. Or, take mallet and chisel and cut out by hand. Takes longer, but works just as well. The gun rack has dowel pegs on its facing edge to retain the gun barrels. Any of several types of locks can be used to lock the cabinet door. Check with your local hardware store. The drawer can be quite handy for storing gun-cleaning materials. Stain and finish as you like. Good hunting!

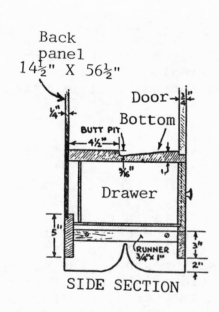

Back panel
14½" X 56½"

Door
Bottom
¾"
¼"
BUTT PIT
4½"
⁹⁄₁₆"
Drawer
5"
3"
2"
RUNNER ¾"x 1"

SIDE SECTION

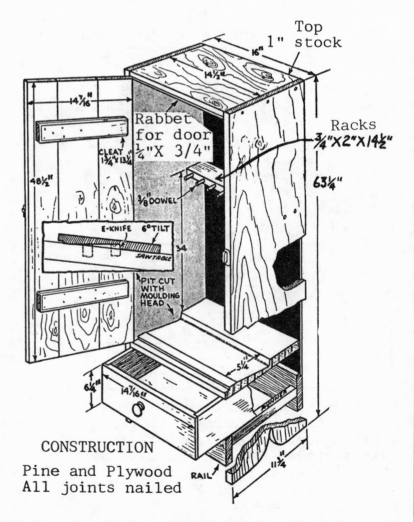

Top
1" stock
16"
14½"
14³⁄₁₆"
Rabbet for door ¼"X ¾"
Racks
¾"X2"X14½"
CLEAT 1¾"x13¼"
48½"
⅛"DOWEL
63¼"
E-KNIFE 6°TILT
SAW TABLE
¾
PIT CUT WITH MOULDING HEAD
5¼"
6¼"
14⁷⁄₁₆"
RUNNER
RAIL
11¼"

CONSTRUCTION
Pine and Plywood
All joints nailed

## MINI OVENS

The next time that you want to roast potatoes in an open campfire, put them into empty tin cans and they won't burn so much. The tin cans make excellent Mini Ovens.

## SOOT BE-GONE

Campers and backpackers, remember this little trick and it will make cleaning of outdoor cooking utensils a whole lot easier. Just rub down the bottoms of the utensils with liquid detergent in advance. Allow to dry on. Later soot will wash off easily.

### BUREAUCRAT'S LAW

The more stupid the idea, the more possible it is.

## WATER "TOTE"

Pointed end    Branch cut from bush

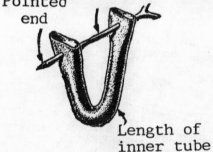

Length of inner tube

For you campers and backpackers, a length of old auto inner tube is a lot less bulky to carry than a bucket. It folds to a small packet, yet when submerged in a stream and both ends scooped up at the same time, carries as much water as a bucket. Jam a pointed stick thru both ends for easy carrying. Keep one in the trunk of your car for emergencies.

Confucius say:

Man without <u>Poor Man's Catalog</u> is like pigeon about to be plucked!

## POOR MAN'S MINI KITCHEN

Back in the good old days, camping out usually meant roughing it in the boondocks. No more, my friend. Nowadays folks mostly "rough it" in comfort. Campers, mobile homes, and even vans can be seen "roughing it" everyday in camping parks across the country. But once in a while, a family or party of campers will decide to backpack out into the boonies--perhaps out on a hunting or fishing trip. And this is where our little, portable Mini Kitchen will come into its own. While it doesn't provide the modern conveniences of a home kitchen, it does provide the answer to the problem of a place for everything. The compact cabinet is designed to hold eating utensils, a cooking kit, and enough canned and dehydrated foods to feed six people for a week. It is easy to transport as the legs are removable, allowing it to fit neatly into the trunk of even a compact car. But what our camp cook (my wife) likes about it is the convenience of everything in one place, and the drop lid that provides a useful worktable.

As shown in the drawings, the Mini Kitchen is simply a wooden box with legs, and quite simple to build. Keep the cost down by using scrap wood.

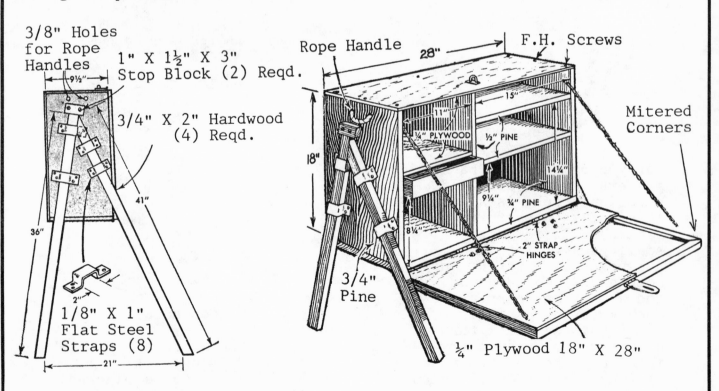

## BEER CAN HOOK REMOVER

## BAIT KEEPER

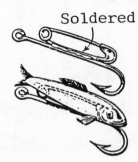

Soldered

## TENNIS RACQUET FISH NET

When some big lunker swallows the hook, a beer can opener makes an excellent hook remover. Matter-of-fact, that's what I told my wife it was made for. Just slip the eye of the hook through the rear of the opener as shown. Then slide the end of the opener down into the bend of the hook. The bend in the end of the opener provides leverage to work hook loose. You will find this hook-removing tool on all good boats.

If you have a problem keeping live bait on your hook, try this little gem. Solder a safety pin to a long shank hook. To use, you open the pin and impale the bait on it. Then just close it. Even the sneakiest fish will not be able to remove it without becoming your dinner.

Lots of tennis folks are switching to the new aluminum tennis raquets. This leaves a lot of the old wood racquets with nothing to do. By sawing off the wooden handle about 8" back from the round frame, buying a cheap fish net, and attaching to the frame with the nylon cord from the X tennis racquet, you have a neat fishing net. Thanks, and a tip-o-the hat to Barbara Anderson for this one.

You got him now, Rich! He's tiring, don't let him get away boy!

# POOR MAN'S FISH LURES

**SPOON FOR BASS AND PIKE**

Punch Holes

Cut from tablespoon

PIKE SPOON →

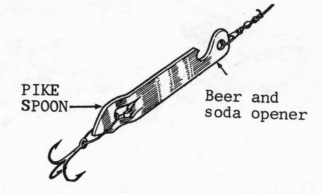

Beer and soda opener

**FUZZY BUG**
Made from a pipe cleaner.
Put a little head cement
on this, rub it in sand,
and it looks just like a
hatchery food pellet. And
WOW, you should see them
flock to it!

**PAN FISH MINNOW**
Punch holes

Cut from coffee can

**WOBBLING MINNOW**

Cut from the plastic handle of old toothbrush

**CLOTHESPIN BASS CATCHER**

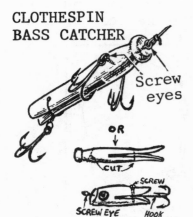

Screw eyes

OR

CUT

SCREW

SCREW EYE    HOOK

Paint in
eyes, and
you have a
Clothes Plug!

Lookout fish!

**PAPER-CLIP JIGS**

**RUBBERBAND WIGGLERS**

Fishing lures, like everything else,
are going up in price. But the Poor
fisher Man can both beat the cost and
still tell tall tales, by designing
his own lures from common materials.

**POOR MAN'S usual catch!**

## POOR MAN'S FEMALE FEATHER FLETCHER

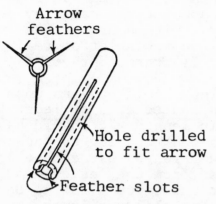

Arrow feathers

Hole drilled to fit arrow

Feather slots

Trying to hold newly glued feathers on an arrow is for the birds. Build this simple jig from a drilled-out wooden dowel. Drill lengthwise to fit over arrow. Cut three equally spaced slots to hold feathers. Coat entire jig with paraffin to prevent glue from adhering to it. Insert glue-dipped feathers into slots and allow to dry. If you need to ask about the name, you're too young to be reading this book. Or too old!

## GOLF BALL CLEANER

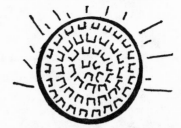

An old golf ball that has been used hard and is dirty, is sometimes hard to find on the fairway. Just soak it overnight in a solution of ¼ cup household ammonia and 1 cup water. It will come out bright and clean, making it easy to find.

"This country has come to feel the same when Congress is in session as when the baby gets hold of a hammer!"
                    Will Rogers

Wow! A turf birdie!

## CAMPFIRE STARTER

Sometimes it can be quite a job to try and start a campfire on a windy day. It can be done easily if you arrange your dry kindling and balls of paper inside a paper bag. Place the bag with its mouth out of the wind and put your match inside bag.

## INDOOR TARGET RANGE

Just the thing for a cold winter evening--an indoor target range can provide you with hours of fun, plus give you a lot of real rifle target practice.

You should have an unobstructed area at least 40' in length. It should have a door leading to the target range that can be locked from the inside. And, of course, you allow no one near the target cabinet when in use. When training children in the use of firearms, they should always be under adult supervision. Check local ordinances governing the use of firearms in the home before building this target range.

IMPORTANT:    This target cabinet is designed for use with low-caliber firearms only! Do Not use with high-powered firearms!

The target cabinet is cut out of 3/4" plywood. The sides, front, back, and bottom panels are all attached to 1" X 3" lumber uprights with wood screws. Before the front panel is attached, a 6" X 8 3/4" target cutout is made in it. Heavy-gauge, galvanized sheet metal is nailed to the inside sides, back, bottom, and halfway up the front panel. The entire inside surface of the wood cabinet, except for the top half of the front panel, should be covered with this heavy-gauge sheet metal. Both side panels are cut with a 45° angle to hold the 3/8"-thick steel plate top. This steel plate deflects the bullets down into the sand stored inside the cabinet. The cabinet, when finished and placed in position, must be filled at least half-full of sand. This sand should be banked from front to rear. A steel supply company can provide the steel plate to size.

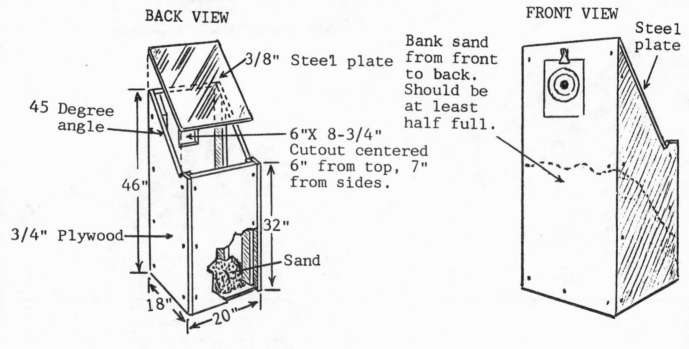

BACK VIEW

3/8" Steel plate

45 Degree angle

6"X 8-3/4" Cutout centered 6" from top, 7" from sides.

46"

32"

3/4" Plywood

Sand

18"

20"

FRONT VIEW

Bank sand from front to back. Should be at least half full.

Steel plate

## KNIFE-SHARPENING SHEATH

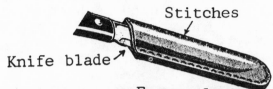

Stitches

Knife blade

Emery cloth stitched between two layers of felt

Emery cloth →

← Felt

Keep your sheath knife sharp and rust-free in this abrasive-lined sheath. Stitch a piece of fine abrasive cloth between two layers of 1/8" felt. Use nylon fish line for long life. Sheath must be sized for snug fit around blade so abrasive will hone cutting edge when blade is inserted and withdrawn. On occasion, put a few drops of light oil on the felt to prevent rust.

## POOR MAN'S BAILING PUMP

As you can plainly see, there is nothing fancy about this. A plumbers force cup with a hole drilled in the side for a small plastic hose. Push hose in until tip is flush with cup edge. Cement in place and you got it. I got the idea from a rich man's yacht. Everything leaks!

## POOR MAN'S DRIVE-EM-CRAZY PLUG

Holes

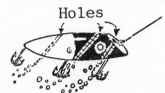

I suppose every fisherman has had those days when nothing works. No matter what tempting bait you toss on the waters, the big lunker just won't go for it. Here is the bait of last resort. Take any old, wooden or plastic plug and convert it into a real popping bait. Drill at least three ¼" holes ½" apart diagonally through the body of the plug. These holes cause the plug to pop and gurgle, leaving a trail of bubbles which drives big lunkers right out of their minds. If he don't strike, look for another spot, cause he ain't home!

Say pal, loan me five and I'll pay you back when my ship comes in.

Looks to me, Sir, more like your ship sank with you still on it!

© 1980 VOLK

# POOR MAN'S FLY-TYING VISE

Anyone who has tried tying their own fishing flies without a vise knows that you gotta have at least three hands to do the job. By mounting a pair of ordinary pliers on a wooden base you can make an excellent fly-tying vise. Drill aligning holes through both handles of the pliers to take a (thin) bolt. A compression spring is slipped over the bolt to hold the handles of the pliers apart. A wing nut is turned on the bolt to lock the pliers closed around the hook. Blind holes are drilled into the wooden base to receive the ends of the handles and to hold the pliers upright. The distance between these drilled holes is determined by the size of the pliers used. Holes should be slightly larger than required to allow for adjustment of the compression spring. Just tighten the wing nut to clamp the jaws over the hook you are fly tying. Try to use as small a diameter bolt as possible through the plier's handles so they will not be weakened and still can be used for ordinary use. A 1/8" wood dowel is set into the wooden base to hold the thread spool. A small section of screen door spring serves as a holder for loose ends of thread. Just mount the spring between two small wooden brackets as shown. Drill out the wooden brackets to accept each end of the screen door spring and hold it in position. Both screen door and compression spring should be available at your local hardware store. And may the flies you tie always grab the biggest lunkers in the lake!

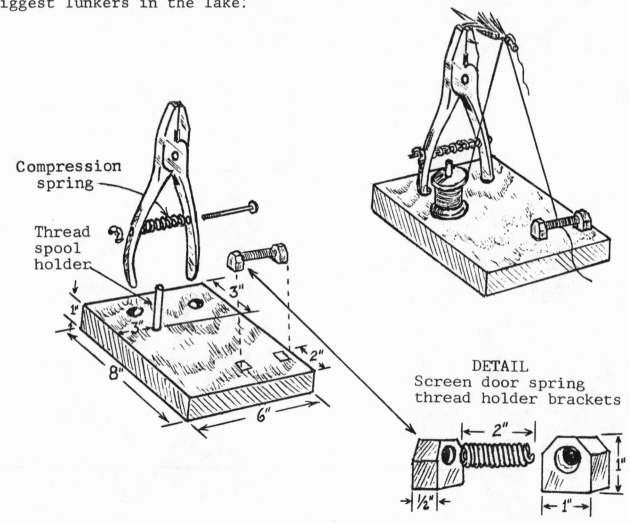

Compression spring

Thread spool holder

3"

3"

1"

8"

6"

2"

DETAIL
Screen door spring
thread holder brackets

2"

½"

1"

1"

## CAR OWNER'S LAW

Your car will only run out of gas at least ten miles from the nearest gasoline station, and it will be closed!

## FIRE STARTER

If you have ever tried to start a wet-wood campfire with a match, you know what fire-starting problems can be. A used shotgun-shell filled with melted paraffin and a string wick makes for a great wet-wood fire starter.

## DECOY DUCKS

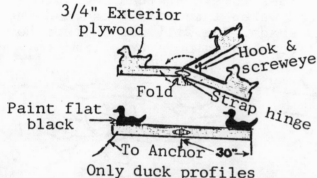

3/4" Exterior plywood

Fold

Hook & screweye

Strap hinge

Paint flat black

To Anchor 30"

Only duck profiles are visible in water.

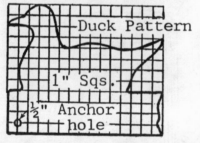

Duck Pattern

1" Sqs.

½" Anchor hole

For the duck hunter who doesn't like messing with a load of bulky decoys or fussing with the trappings of setting them out (or even the price of replacing the things), have we got good news for you! A little scrap 3/4" exterior plywood, a few 4" strap hinges, and a jigsaw, and you can turn out as many "shadow" decoys as you can use in one evening. Use pattern to trace profiles. The same pattern serves for all ducks. Saw out base strips 4" X 30" long, and attach two rear strips to front one with strap hinges. Place hook and screw-eye between to back strips so when hooked, it will lock them at any angle between 45º and 90º. Drill hole for anchor. Use only flat paint for ducks. Any glossy paint will scare away keen-vision real ducks. Decoys simply fold flat when not in use.

## TABLE-TENNIS WALL CADDY

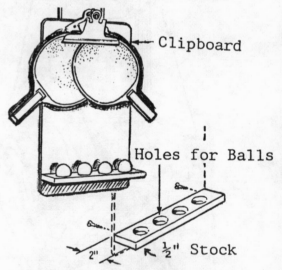

Clipboard

Holes for Balls

2"

½" Stock

Table tennis buffs will find this little Wall Caddy just the thing for keeping track of paddles and balls. Just mount a wall rack to an ordinary clipboard. Slip the paddles under the clip and you can always find them.

## PORTABLE FIELD COOLER

For the camper, hunter, or fisherman who takes perishables out into the field, this little Field Cooler is just the ticket. Build from any type of 5-gal. metal container that has been thoroughly cleaned. Install hardware shelves with sheet-metal screws, then cover the entire outside of the can with heavy flannel or an old cotton blanket--any material that will absorb water easily. Sew this covering together as tightly as possible around the can. Make a flap to cover the opening. Make sure that you have punched all required holes in the container before covering! Take a 2-lb. coffee can and punch a hole dead center in the bottom. Make four small splits in sides for lamp wicks. Sew wicks to cloth covering. Pour cold water into coffee can and over the container. Hang in the shade. You will not believe how cool your perishables will keep. Hang on a tree limb to keep critters out.

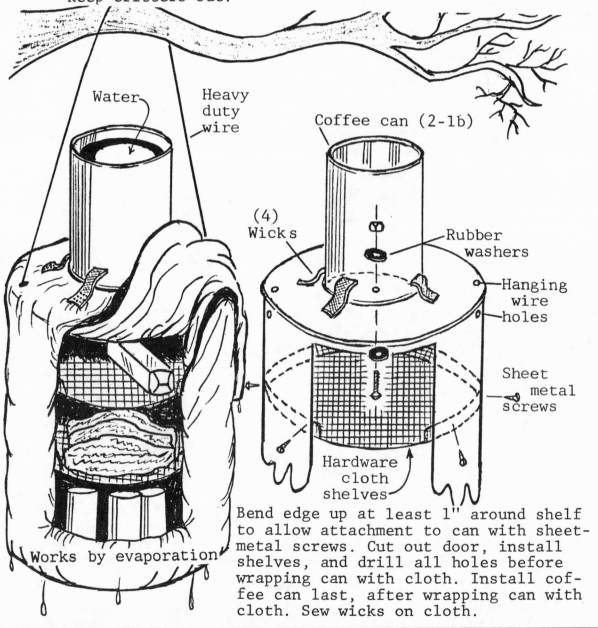

Water

Heavy duty wire

Coffee can (2-lb)

(4) Wicks

Rubber washers

Hanging wire holes

Sheet metal screws

Hardware cloth shelves

Works by evaporation

Bend edge up at least 1" around shelf to allow attachment to can with sheet-metal screws. Cut out door, install shelves, and drill all holes before wrapping can with cloth. Install coffee can last, after wrapping can with cloth. Sew wicks on cloth.

## ARROWHEAD SHEATH

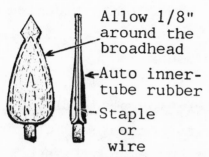

Allow 1/8" around the broadhead

Auto inner-tube rubber

Staple or wire

It's easy to make guards for sharp, hunting, broadhead arrows. Trace the outline of the broadhead on a section of old inner-tube rubber, adding at least 1/8" all around the outline. Cut two pieces to shape, then roughen and clean as when patching a tube. Apply rubber cement around outer edges for a weatherproof seal. Then staple or wire bottom edges as shown.

## CAMPFIRE TRIPOD

Hole for hook

One old tin can, three green sticks, and a coat hanger wire gives you a a foolproof tripod. Make sure the three stick ends are wedged securely inside can. Punch hole in side of can for wire hook.

## POOR MAN'S TEASPOON MOLD

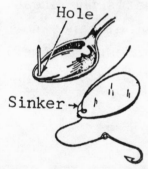

Hole

Sinker

Along with everything else, lead sinkers are going up in price. But, using an old teaspoon you can beat this game. Drill a small hole near the tip of the spoon. Then press a small nail through the hole from the underside. Must be a snug fit. Pour molten lead into spoon and allow to harden. Pull out nail with pliers and tap lead from spoon. Instant sinker!

## LAWYER'S LAW

Prevent someone from getting your client's money, while you have your hand in their pocket!

Here you go, Doc, operate on it with this one!

## UNUSUAL CONTESTS

Talk about seeing the feathers fly! Ever see a chicken-plucking contest?
Would you believe four women once plucked a total of twelve chickens in
sixty-seven seconds to set a world's record. How about a cow-chip throwing contest? Could you break the record of 176 feet 10 inches? Don't
like cow-chips? Well then, how about a watermelon seed-spitting contest?
The record here is 54 feet 10 inches. Just pucker up and let her go! Perhaps you would rather go see a pancake race, or even a fishworm judging
contest. All of these, and many more, have been captured in a book by another friend of ours--Vince Luciani of Egg Harbor City, NJ.  Vince is an
electrical engineer who also writes and runs his own small publishing
business part time. He sent me a copy of "Guide to Unusual Contests in
America" and I enjoyed it so much, I thought I should pass the good news
along. The book describes in detail a whole bootle of wacky and unusual
contests held across the USA. It has many pictures and gives the dates
and locations of each contest (just in case you would like to take a low-
cost, "Poor Man's" vacation and see some real Americana in action). Don't
take any foreign visitors though, otherwise they will know what they only
suspected before--that we're all crazy! Vince, I already got my own all
picked out. No sense in anyone else even showing up. That's the Great
Beer Belly Contest. I can win the "sexiest belly" division, hands down!
If you would like your own copy of "Guide to Unusual Contests in America,"
send $4.95 plus $1.00 postage to: Cologne Press, P.O. Box 682, Cologne,
NJ 08213.

Mirror, mirror, on the wall who's got the sexiest belly of all?

# Woodworking

The power tool projects shown below are not available in <u>this</u> catalog. They are available in our self-published Poor Man's Catalog #5.

If you think that's bad, you should see him swat flies with his shotgun!

Build a better mouse trap, and the world will beat a path to your door.

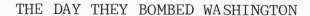

THE DAY THEY BOMBED WASHINGTON

Growing up in Washington, D.C., during World War II was a thrilling experience. I can still remember the great air attack on the city by German bombers--something most folks don't know about due to security at
the time. But I remember, and so does a certain mounted Park Police officer who patrolled Rock Creek Park where the Washington Zoo is located.
In fact, I bet he never forgets it! The story goes something like this:
Back when I was about twelve years old (a thousand years ago) our big
thing was building flying model airplanes. Every spare moment between
school and my paper route was spent carefully cutting, forming, and glu-
ing small strips of balsa wood into airplane models. With the war going
on, my friends and I spent many happy hours building and flying exact
models of war planes. We flew them in our yards, on the street, in the
parks, and anywhere else that we could keep them out of the trees. But
no matter how careful we were, sooner or later they ended up in a tree
or bush. Once they got too beat up to patch or repair, we had a special
ending for them. We would take them to the nearby Calvert Street bridge
(over one hundred feet high) which spanned Rock Creek Park in Washington,
and there we would plant a fire cracker into the beatup old model plane.
Then we would fly it off the bridge with the fire cracker lit. We would
wind up the rubberband motor, tape the wing flaps up (so it would gain
altitude), light the fire cracker, and let her fly. Usually the plane
would fly out forty or fifty yards, then blow up when the fire cracker
went off. It would then make a spectacular crash into the ground, over
one hundred feet below.

A friend of mine spent weeks building a huge model of a German Stuka
dive bomber. The wing span was over three feet long-- a really big
model for those days. The day finally came when my friend decided it

was time for its final flight. It had been patched one too many times. When we got to the bridge we were pretty excited, as this was by far the largest plane we had ever flown off the bridge. Since it was so big, we decided to use a cherry bomb rather than our usual fire cracker, figuring that the cherry bomb had at least three times the power of our little fire crackers, and should be able to do the blowup with a bang! In order to allow a long flight, we attached a cast-off cigarette butt to the cherry-bomb fuse, which in effect gave it a slow fuse. My friend wound up the rubberband motor while I checked the roadway running under the bridge for approaching cars. I yelled "All clear" and the plane was launched into the wild blue.

In our excitement we had forgotten to tape the wing flaps up, but the plane was flying straight and level. About this time, I noticed a Park Police officer had just ridden his horse from one of the many trails in Rock Creek Park out onto the roadway. He was about 75 yards off, slowly riding towards the bridge, minding his own business. He hadn't spotted either my friend and me, up on the bridge, or the airplane. When the plane was about fifty yards away it hit a strong downdraft and banked towards the left and the roadway. Then it turned nose down and went into a steep dive. The sudden dive somehow shook loose our cherry bomb which was now falling at an angle towards the roadway. You could see the fuse sparkling as it went down. The diving plane suddenly hit a powerful updraft causing it to pull out of its dive and level off at just above tree-top level. It was now heading directly for the unsuspecting Park Police officer and his horse. The officer and his horse were less than sixty yards from the bridge when the cherry bomb went off with a flash and roar, right over the roadway. The sound echoed under the big bridge making a tremendous boom! A large cloud of gray and white smoke appeared just above the roadway. The Park Police officer and his horse were now fully alert. I could tell, because his horse had jumped four feet straight up into the air, and the police officer was hanging on for dear life to the saddle. Now, I don't know what the police officer was thinking at this point, but when his horse saw that big German Stuka dive bomber coming right at him, I know what he thought! Have you ever seen a horse stand up on its hind legs and do a perfect 180-degree turn? I bet that police officer had never seen it either, because he landed on his backside in the grass beside the road, while his horse took off galloping back down the road. Then the amazed officer looked up and saw a

German dive bomber flash by over his head and disappear over the tree tops. I would have given twenty bucks to have heard that police officer explain how he lost his horse, on the day they bombed Washington.

THE POOR MAN

EXPERIENCE IS A HARD TEACHER. IT GIVES THE TEST FIRST, AND THE LESSON AFTERWARDS.

RAISED CUTTING BOARD

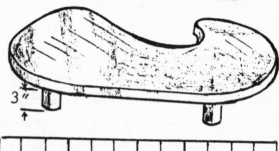

3"

DOWEL SHELVES

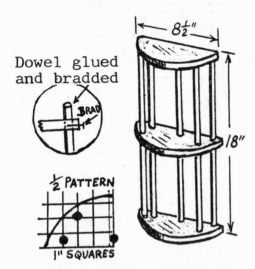

Dowel glued and bradded

BRAD

8½"

18"

½ PATTERN

1" SQUARES

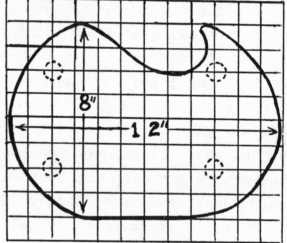

8"

1 2"

1" Squares

Five 3/8" X 18" dowels and three "half moon" cuts of ½" plywood can give you some attractive bric-a-brac shelves. Cut shelves from plywood and stack to drill all dowel holes at one time. Glue and brad all dowels to each shelf. Finish as desired.

The kitchen cutting board is one of the easiest and most inexpensive wood projects that you can build. They make great gifts. Use 3/4" hardwood stock for the board. We used 1¼" dowel stock for legs, which are glued in place. Rub in a coating of salad oil to finish.

# DO-ANYTHING DESK

We originally built this little desk as a handy telephone desk. Then the kids discovered that it made a neat homework desk. Our daughter found that it was just the right height for her typewriter. And now our eldest is eyeing it as a great place for his computer terminal. So, whatever you do, don't plan on building and using it yourself. It'll never happen!

Build from 3/4" pine lumber. A 1" wood dowel goes through all of the shelves, but only ¼" into the top. All shelves and the drawer rails are screwed to the side by counter-boring deep enough for the screw head to be covered with a wood plug. The top is blind mortised to fit into the tongues of the sides. The top is glued into place. The drawer construction is conventional with the sides made of ½" stock and the bottom ¼" plywood. Sand it down lightly and it's ready to stain or paint the color of your choice.

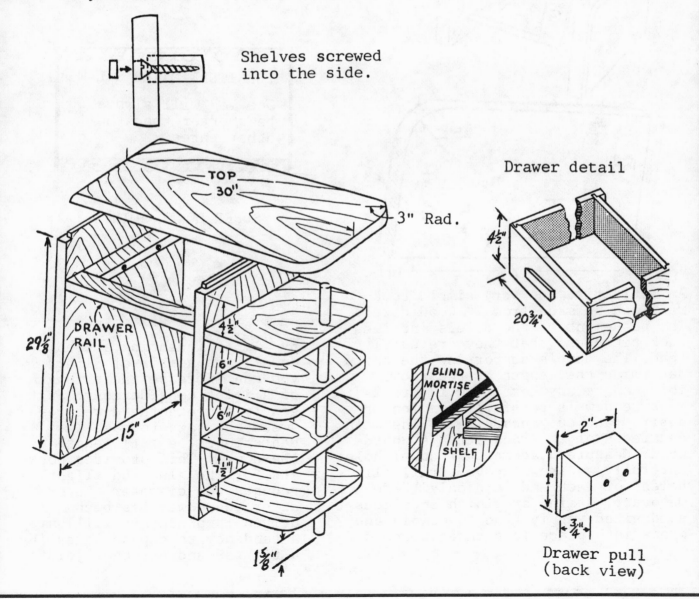

Shelves screwed into the side.

Drawer detail

TOP 30"

3" Rad.

DRAWER RAIL

29⅛"

15"

4½"

6"

6"

7½"

1⅝"

4½"

20¾"

BLIND MORTISE

SHELF

2"

1"

¾"

Drawer pull (back view)

## SHARPEN-A-DOWEL

One of those little dime-store pencil sharpeners makes a nice, neat, quick chamfer on the ends of small dowels.

## DOWEL BOOK RACK

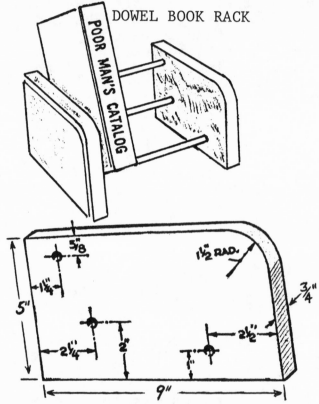

An attractive but very simple book rack can be made from ½" wood dowels. The placement of the dowels inclines book titles so that they are easily read. The dowels supporting the books determine the length of the rack. This can be anywhere from 12" to 24". Measure dowels carefully for length desired and cut accordingly. The main endpieces of the rack are 3/4" hardwood. Measure placement of dowel holes carefully as shown above. Drill all holes for each endpiece only ½" deep. Decorate, stain, or finish endpieces as desired. Apply glue to dowels and press into place in each endpiece.

## COOK-A-DOWEL

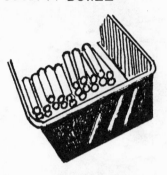

If you will heat wooden dowels in a low to medium warm oven before using, you will drive out moisture. Later, after you have used them, the wood will reabsorb moisture from the air and expand, making for a much tighter joint.

---

### FURNITURE MAKER'S LAW

One leg will always be shorter than the other three.

---

## SUPER DOWEL JOINTS

By simply indenting a wood dowel with a pair of pliers you can increase the strength of a joint considerably. Just gently squeeze the dowel between the jaws to make indentations the full length of the dowel. This provides pockets for the glue and slightly reduces the diameter. Later, after the dowel has been driven in place, it will have a tendency to expand, creating a tighter and stronger joint.

# APPLIANCE HOLDER

This little Appliance Holder can handle anything from a toaster oven to an electric hot pot, and keep them up and out of the way. Helps to keep your kitchen counter from getting cluttered up with appliances.

Better yet, it makes a great one-evening project that can be built from scraps found around your shop. Built as shown, it uses no hardware of any type. Use 3/4" stock all around, with ¼" X 1½" wood dowels to hold it together.

Mark all holes to be drilled in sides and back first. Carefully drill ¼" holes, then place shelf in position and mark through the predrilled holes in sides and back. Make sure all holes are centered before drilling. Put a tad of white glue on the tip of each wood dowel before driving in place.

Add a row of cup hooks screwed into the bottom below shelf, and you can hang coffee cups, kitchen tools, or colorful pot holders. Depending upon the stock used, paint, or finish natural using a good grade of varnish. Take care to hang on wall securely.

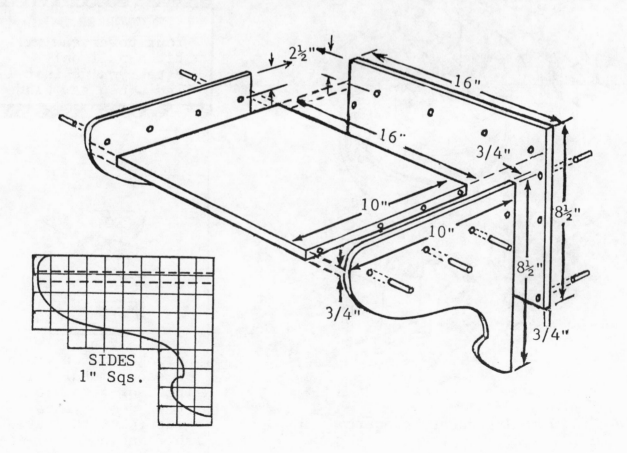

SIDES
1" Sqs.

124

## GLUE GRABBER
Small punched holes

If you have a problem getting a mortise-and-tenon joint to hold, roughen the surface of both the mortise and tenon before assembling. Use an ice pick, or any sharp, pointed instrument. Prick the surface of the wood with many small indentations into which the glue will work and form a strong bond.

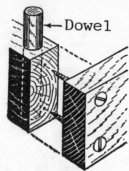

We're looking for a poor politician. Anybody ever seen one? We've given up looking for an honest one!

## END GRAIN HOLDER

← Dowel

Screws driven into end grain are notorious for easily pulling loose. Drill a hole parallel to the end of the piece in such a position that the screws will enter it when driven. Press a wood dowel into the hole and drive screws into it.

### WOODWORKER'S LAW
Your power saw will hit a nail only after you've installed a new saw blade.

Speed'n, wrecking county property, an litter'n the hi-way. You in a heap a trouble, boy!

## SOLID JOINTS

Sprinkle a few grains of sand, metal filings, or shreds of steel wool over a glue joint to prevent shifting under clamping pressure and to make a stronger joint.

## POOR MAN'S DOWEL FURNITURE

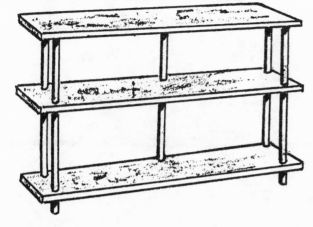

You can save a bunch of bucks and build solid, serviceable furniture that will probably outlast you, using common wooden dowels and ordinary hand tools. Wooden dowels of assorted sizes allow quick and easy assembly of a number of useful furniture accessories. Both the bookcase and step table shown here use only wood and dowels. No hardware, not even nails, are required to build. Both pieces are constructed exactly the same way using the small ¼" X 3" wood dowels driven into pre-drilled holes at all joints. Both plans are expandable, and can be changed to suit your needs.

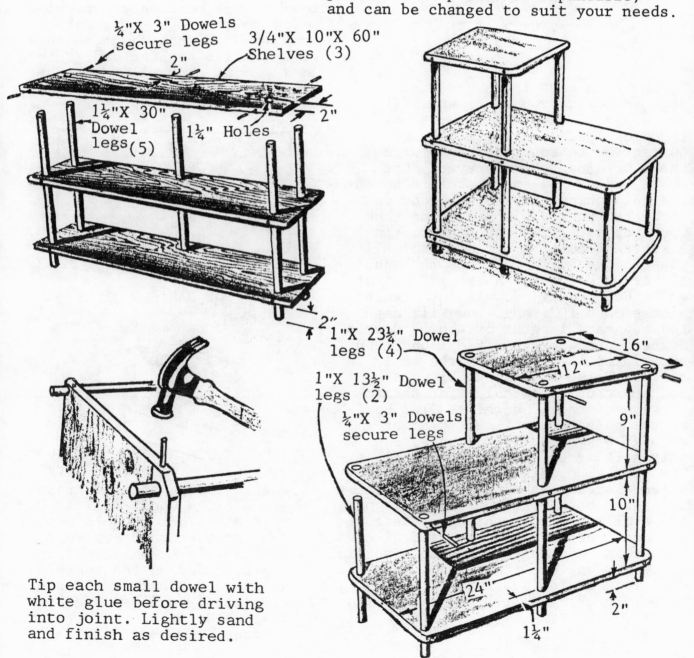

¼"X 3" Dowels secure legs

3/4"X 10"X 60" Shelves (3)

2"

1¼"X 30" Dowel legs (5)

1¼" Holes

2"

2"

1"X 23¼" Dowel legs (4)

1"X 13½" Dowel legs (2)

¼"X 3" Dowels secure legs

16"

12"

9"

10"

24"

2"

1¼"

Tip each small dowel with white glue before driving into joint. Lightly sand and finish as desired.

## POOR MAN'S BUBBLY RACK

So who said anything about wine? You store what you want, and I'll store my own knee-slapping, floor-thumping, head-bashing home brew. Guaranteed to snap your eyes wide open. Or close them forever! Just don't take a few snorts before building this thing, or you will end up with the funniest looking wine rack you ever saw. Mine ended up looking like the leaning tower of Pisa! All you need to build this are 1¼" and ½" hardwood dowels--about 12 feet of each. Cut the 1¼" dowels into twelve pieces each 10" long. You will need two separate lengths of the ½" dowels. Sixteen pieces each 3 5/8" long, and six pieces 12" long. Now the real fun begins. Using a ½" spade bit, mark and start drilling holes for the insertion of the ½" dowels. NOTE: Horizontal holes are drilled straight through six of the 1¼" dowels, and only halfway through the other six. The long ½" dowels fit through these holes. For the other six 1¼" dowels, all holes both vertical and horizontal are drilled halfway through. These are the end sections. Lightly sand all pieces and assemble with glue, checking all right angles with a steel square. And, if you didn't drink before you started this, you will before you finish!

## POOR MAN'S SANDING DISKS

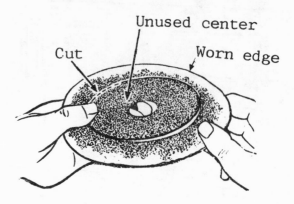

Most sanding disks can have two lives. You can salvage the little-used center portion by trimming off the worn edge. This makes a smaller disk that should be used on a smaller sanding pad. This little mini disk will give just as good service as the original.

> ### YOU
> are living in the good old days that your grandchildren will hear so much about.

## POOR MAN'S V-BLOCK

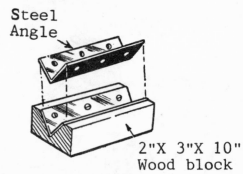

When drilling holes in round stock (like wood dowels) you need a V-Block to hold stock. You can make your own Poor Man's style by making right angle cuts down the center of a hardwood block. A 10" section of angle iron is screwed to the inside of block for a true surface. Wow! How do we do it?

FIDDLE-BACK FOOT STOOL

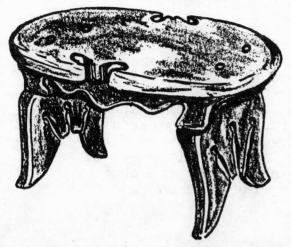

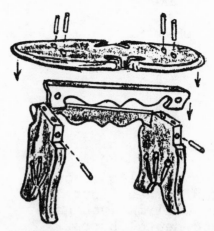

Dowel pins are driven through
the top and into the ends to
strengthen the joints.

For those lovers of early Colonial pieces, here is the famed Fiddle-Back
Foot Stool. The original stool after which this reproduction was patter-
ned is a survivor of early Colonial days. Like many of those early pieces
its beauty never wears out. The stool should be made from 1" stock, preferably maple. The side rails can be planed down to 7/8", but the balance
of the stock should be planed only enough for smoothness. Keep in mind
that the original piece was crafted using only hand tools. Lay out the
pattern using 1" graph squares. Each pattern need only be one-half of the
design as it's then turned over and traced onto the wood to complete the
design. Saw the wood by hand or on a jig, band, or sabre saw. The top of
the stool is shaped to resemble the body of a violin. File and sand the
edge of the top and the lower edges of the end pieces to simulate wear.
Bevel the top edge of each end board to make the ends splay out. Then
bevel the bottom edges to make them rest evenly on the floor. Assemble
the side rails to the end boards first, using a quality glue. Reinforce
by drilling a hole at each joint and inserting 7/16" X 2" wood dowel pins.
The top is secured to the end boards by using two dowels inserted through
the top into each end. Sand the dowel heads and holes smooth. Finish with
maple stain, then wax thoroughly. Built as directed, you should be able
to turn this over to your grandchildren as an heirloom.

1" SQUARES                    &                    END BOARD (2)

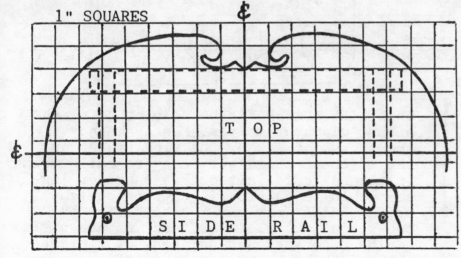

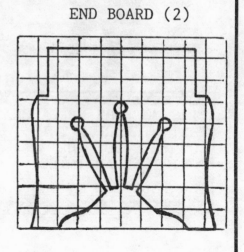

128

## ADOPT A DENTIST

Pay your dental bill on time and perhaps your dentist will let you have his used dental burrs. Chucked into a high-speed hand grinder they make very nice intricate wood carvings. If your dentist won't cooperate, you might hint that your payment may be delayed. Of course, you don't want to do this until he is finished working on you. Otherwise, you could find your mouth wired shut and braces on your tonsils!

> IT'S NOT THE BUREAUCRACY THAT WILL RUIN THIS COUNTRY, BUT THE POLITICAL APOINTEE!
>
> The Poor Man

## POOR MAN'S COLLET

Those little hand grinders are nice. Especially for very close work. However, I have a bad habit of losing those tiny accessories collets. Then I discovered that hollow rivets will work just as well. Just select a rivet of the right size, split one side, and insert into the chuck. Works like a champ!

## COLONIAL PIPE OR KNIFE RACK

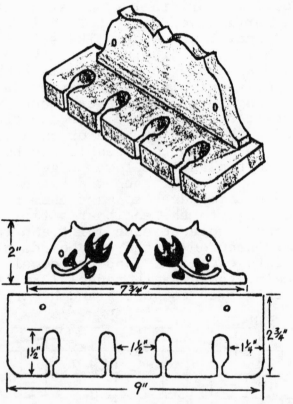

This little rack can be adapted to accept either pipes or knives. Makes a handy accessory for either the pipe smoker or the kitchen. It is very easy to build using just hand tools, although a sabre or jigsaw would be helpful in cutting out the parts. Build from any ½" stock. The back can be cut out plain or fancy as shown. It can be decorated and painted, or finished natural. Makes a real nice gift.

# U-BUILD CARVING TOOLS

The woodcarver and modelmaker can easily make their own precision carving tools from commonly available materials. Everything from chip carving knives to wood gouges can be made in the home shop at very little cost. In most cases you can use recycled materials and design your own special carving tools at no cost. Using the same methods, you can design and build many special purpose tools for your shop. Heat treating the formed tools to maintain sharp cutting edges can easily be done in the shop using gas or propane fuel tanks. Handles for home-built tools can be made from wooden dowels, or even wooden drawer pulls available at most hardware stores. Old, used files, nails, hacksaw blades, drill rods, bolts, and even old kitchen flatware can supply the raw metal materials required. Just one old coathanger can supply the metal for a mini carving set. Temper the steel wire carefully after hammering into shape and you have a carving set that will last you a long time. And the price is right!

Mini Gouge uses common wooden drawer pull as handle.

Old, used hacksaw blades make excellent wood carving knives. No heat treating required. Just grind cutting edge slowly.

← 3½" →

Hacksaw blade

Fold →

Wrapping paper coated with glue.

Used, inexpensive screwdrivers with plastic handles can be worked into many useful tools. First, anneal the shank to be worked by heating til cherry red and cooling slowly. Work into shape desired then reheat til cherry red and quench in oil.

COMBINATION NAIL PULLERS & WIRE STRIPPERS    BRAD PULLER    PRY BAR    SCREW EYE DRIVER    COTTER PIN PULLER

½" Dowel 4½" long

File groove

2"
1"RAD.
1/16"  ← 1¼" →
2"
5/8"RAD.
1/16"  ← 1" →
1"RAD.
5/64"
45°
← 2" →
3/8"
5/16"
1"RAD.  ← 1 3/32" →

End profiles

Side profiles

Scoring saw

Wood carving chisels, gouges, and skews in many different variations and sizes can be made from 1/8" drill rod available from any hardware store. Or consider using old umbrella ribs. They make excellent mini carving tools. The umbrella ribs must first be softened to work into shape desired. Heat red hot. File and work to shape. Each shape should be made in duplicate, one with outside, the other with inside, bevel. Harden by reheating red hot and quenching in water. Drill rod is first worked into shape, then hardened. Heat bright red for ½" back from cutting edge then quench in water or oil.

130

You say that you achieved your great wealth through hard work - whose?

Clip and mail to your Congressman

## Help the Unfortunate!

ABOLISH THE IRS!

## COTTER PIN SANDER

A large cotter pin can serve as a holder for wads of steel wool or strips of sandpaper. Just chuck it into your electric drill and you will find it easy to reach and smooth inside and concave surfaces.

## SPACKLE SPARKLE

You can bring out the almost invisible grit marks left by fine sandpaper on finished wood projects by sprinkling a dry powder surfacing compound sparingly on the wood. Distribute it evenly across the grain with a soft cloth. Any scratches will show up as fine, white lines. Repeat the sanding and powdering process until the surface is free of scratches. Now, when stained, painted, or varnished, it should sparkle!

## HIDE-A-NAIL CHIP

In doing some fancy woodwork where you would like to hide nails, just bury them under a gouged-out chip. Use a sharp woodcarving gouge to lift a chip. Save the chip, then drive and set nail in the gouged recess. Glue chip back in place over concealed nail. Carefully wipe away any excess glue, and when stained and finished, try and find the nail. No way, McKay!

# MINI MALLARDS

Fig. 2.

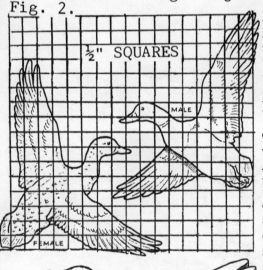

½" SQUARES

MALE

FEMALE

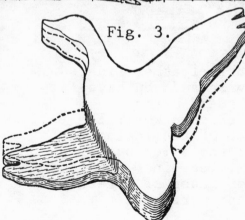

Fig. 3.

Most anateur craftsmen who have a reasonably good eye for proportion and color can hand-carve mini game birds. First, expand the graph below to ½" squares. Then draw in the ducks following the graph grid. Next, lay out your graph drawing on a nice piece of 2" white pine, about 10" wide for one duck. Use your saw to cut out the outline as shown in Fig. 3. Trim away the excess wood from head and wings. Rough sand the head, wings, and body until they follow the contour lines of the duck. This is known as high relief carving and gives the impression of depth and roundness. Fig. 4. just shows the side and front views of the duck's head to aid in carving. Fig. 5. shows how feathers are simulated with either carving tools or an electric burning pencil. Fine sand the entire duck.

To finish, it would be best to find some color plates to copy. These should be available in any library and on some sports magazine covers. Flat oil paints seem to work best. Fig. 6. shows how the ducks can be mounted on a plaque using a ½" wood dowel. We have also mounted ducks on natural wood slabs leaving the bark on around the slab. With a natural finish it makes a great background for the flying duck. The duck in the top left is a female.

Fig. 4.

Fig. 5.

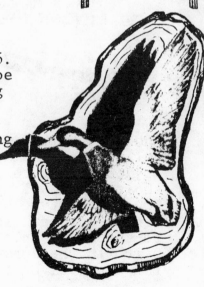

Fig. 6.

## TOY MAKERS LAW

There is no such thing as a child proof toy, and the child that you give it to will prove it.

## POOR BOY'S MUSCLE BUILDER

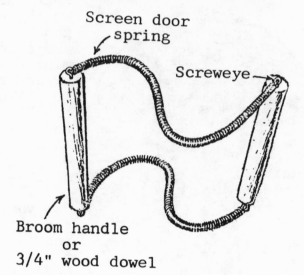

Screen door spring

Screweye

Broom handle
or
3/4" wood dowel

Two ten-inch sections of an old broom handle and two screen door springs with a few screw eyes, and you have a young man's exerciser. Lets him strengthen arm and shoulder muscles.

## SANDING-DISK HOLDER

Cut a paper plate in half, thumbtack both portions to your shop wall, and you have a convient way of storing sanding disks.

## POOR MAN'S EXPANSION PLUG

The next time a wood screw pulls loose from a drawer or door, just roll up a short length of nylon netting of the type used in window screens. Insert into the screw hole, then drive in the screw. Makes for a new tight fit.

## SOFT VISE

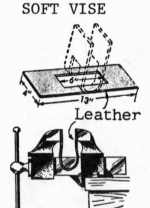

Leather

Install this leather liner in your vise and you have a "soft" guard against marring delicate work. The center cut of the leather fits over the slide bar of your vise. The liner requires no further means of attaching and is easily removed.

# LITTLE FOLKS ROCKER

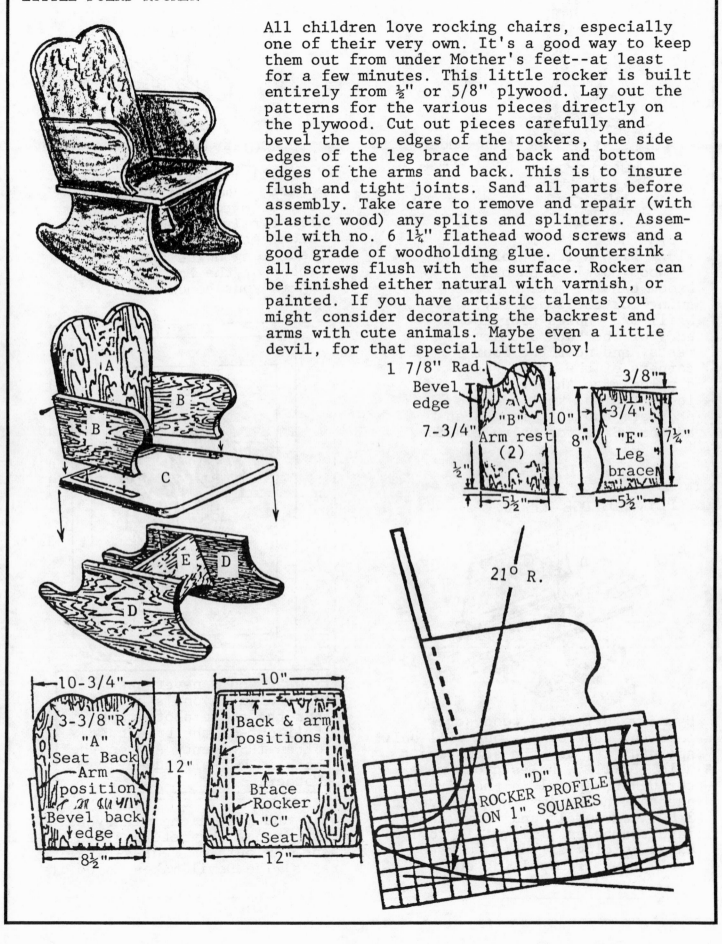

All children love rocking chairs, especially one of their very own. It's a good way to keep them out from under Mother's feet--at least for a few minutes. This little rocker is built entirely from ½" or 5/8" plywood. Lay out the patterns for the various pieces directly on the plywood. Cut out pieces carefully and bevel the top edges of the rockers, the side edges of the leg brace and back and bottom edges of the arms and back. This is to insure flush and tight joints. Sand all parts before assembly. Take care to remove and repair (with plastic wood) any splits and splinters. Assemble with no. 6 1¼" flathead wood screws and a good grade of woodholding glue. Countersink all screws flush with the surface. Rocker can be finished either natural with varnish, or painted. If you have artistic talents you might consider decorating the backrest and arms with cute animals. Maybe even a little devil, for that special little boy!

1 7/8" Rad.
Bevel edge
7-3/4"
"B" Arm rest (2)
10"
½"
5½"

3/8"
3/4"
"E" Leg brace
8"
7¼"
5½"

21° R.

"D" ROCKER PROFILE ON 1" SQUARES

10-3/4"
3-3/8"R.
"A" Seat Back
Arm position
Bevel back edge
12"
8½"

10"
Back & arm positions
Brace
Rocker
"C" Seat
12"

## MINI SWING
## FOR
## SMALL FRY

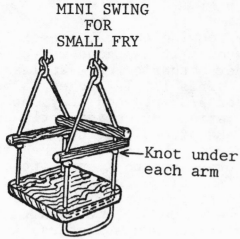

→ Knot under
each arm

A 3/4" board 12" X 14"
along with a length of
1" wood dowel or an old
broom handle, make a great
swing for the small fry.
Drill 3/8" holes near the
ends of the back and arm
rests, and near the four
corners of the seat. Pass
a nylon rope through as
indicated and knot under
each arm about 8" from seat
bottom. Safe for up to 100 lbs.

## PLYWOOD EDGE HOLDER

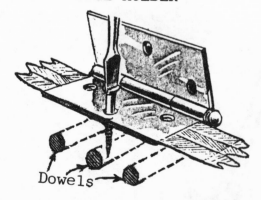

Dowels

Usually, driving a wood screw
into the edge of plywood will only
splinter it, and the screw won't
hold. Drill ¼" holes cross-wise
through the panel in the direct
path of the screws. Apply glue to
3/8" wood dowels and drive them
into the holes. This will provide
extra holding strength to keep
the screws from pulling out.

## MITER BOX HOLDER

Cleat

You will find it a lot
easier to make miter cuts
if your miter box can be
held firmly on your work
bench. Attach a wooden
cleat lengthwise under the
center of the box for clamping in your bench vise.

Now we would never cast
doubts on anyone's ancestry,
but the above photograph
fell out of the briefcase
of an IRS agent. And on the
back it was signed--
Mother!

Clip and mail along with your
next Income Tax return. Then
send for our low rent-a-barrel
rates! The Devil makes us do it.

# TINY TOTS PUZZLES

When you can both amuse children and challenge their imaginations, you have children who are learning. In the modern toy business this is known as the educational toy. We prefer to call it a fun toy, that teaches. The best of these types of toys are ones that children enjoy playing with, while having to make their own decisions. Simple wooden puzzles allow them to do all of this. Best of all, these little wooden puzzles are simple to build and require very little material.

Two pieces of ½" X 9½" X 12" wood stock are required for each puzzle. We prefer solid pine stock and do not recommend plywood. One piece of stock serves as the base, while the other is the cut-out. Lay out, and enlarge the graphs below to ½" squares. Carefully make a reproduction of either the duck or puppy following the drawing in the squares. Bore a small hole just large enough for a jig or coping-saw blade, close to a cutting line so that it won't be noticed. Cut and sand the parts as shown. Sand the cut-out board, then center on the base board and attach with wood screws.

Finish both bases and animals with contrasting colors, making sure to use only non-toxic paints. Eyes are a short wood screw with washer.

TIP: A child's coloring book can give you lots of ideas for cute puzzles like these.

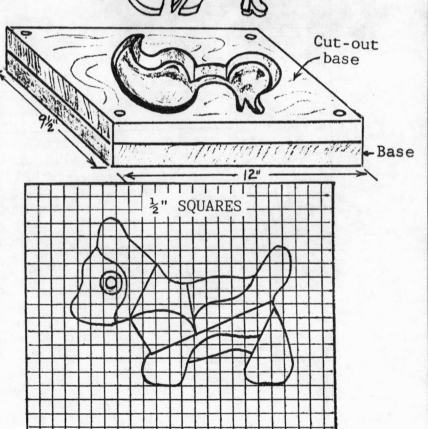

All ½" solid stock

Puzzle parts from cut-out base

Cut-out base

Base

9½"

12"

½" SQUARES

½" SQUARES

I'll never eat another damned peanut.

## PADDLE CLAMP

To avoid bruised or cut fingers when drilling thin stock and having it spin suddenly when the drill bit breaks through, build this simple wooden paddle clamp. Cut out a paddle shaped holder from ½" stock, cut slots and center hole, and install bolts with washers and wing nuts as shown.

## PREVENT NAIL SPLIT

Tighten a C-clamp around the end of a small piece of lumber to prevent splitting the end when nailing.

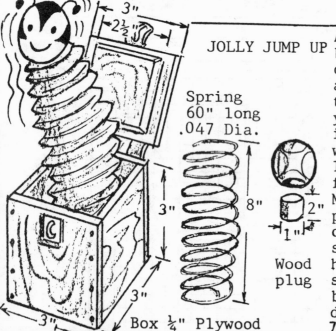

### JOLLY JUMP UP

3"

2½"

Spring
60" long
.047 Dia.

3"

8"

2"

1"

Wood plug

Box ¼" Plywood

A little scrap ¼" plywood, a tennis ball, an old sock or cloth, and 60" of no.047" dia. wire tightly wrapped around a 3/4" pipe to form a spring, then stretched to about 8" long, and you have all the makings for a Jack-in-the-box. First build a 3" square wooden box with a lid hinged with two leather strips. Attach a catch in the front of the box to hold the lid shut. Make a spring by wrapping around a 3/4" pipe, then stretch to 8" Fit cloth or old sock over spring for covering. Cut small circle in bottom of tennis ball head and glue in wooden plug. Staple spring to wooden plug. Paint face and box as desired. Use felt-tip pens to draw in face. Great fun for kids 4 to 74.

## JEEPERS

Using blocks of scrap and wood dowels you can create a small army. Extend the Jeep by another 8" and you have a truck. Make it wider and it can carry equipment.

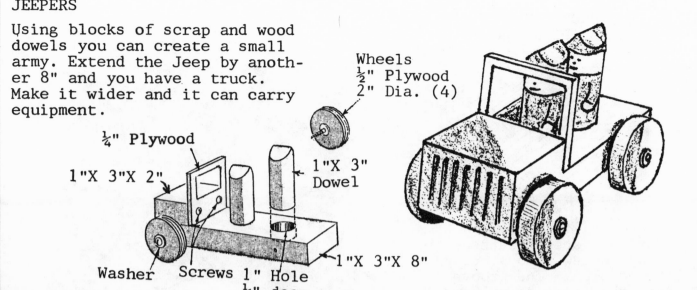

Wheels
½" Plywood
2" Dia. (4)

¼" Plywood

1"X 3"X 2"

1"X 3"
Dowel

Washer    Screws    1" Hole
½" deep

1"X 3"X 8"

## LITTLE PUFF
Made from wood scraps, dowels, and wooden drawer pulls.

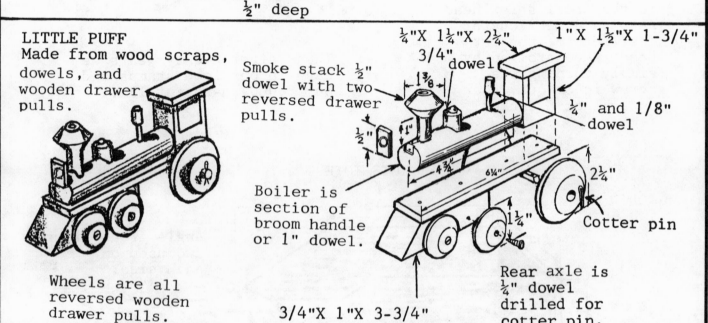

Smoke stack ½" dowel with two reversed drawer pulls.

¼"X 1¼"X 2¼"
3/4" dowel

1"X 1½"X 1-3/4"

¼" and 1/8" dowel

1 3/8"

½"

4¾"

6¼"

2¼"

1¼"

Cotter pin

Boiler is section of broom handle or 1" dowel.

Wheels are all reversed wooden drawer pulls.

3/4"X 1"X 3-3/4"

Rear axle is ¼" dowel drilled for cotter pin.

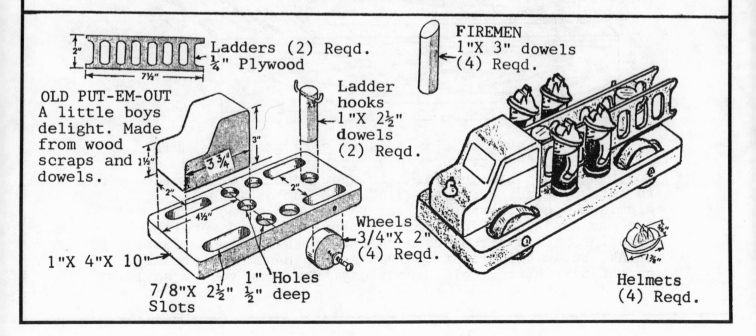

2"

7½"

Ladders (2) Reqd.
¼" Plywood

FIREMEN
1"X 3" dowels
(4) Reqd.

Ladder hooks
1"X 2½" dowels
(2) Reqd.

## OLD PUT-EM-OUT
A little boys delight. Made from wood scraps and 1½" dowels.

3"

3 3/4"

2"

4½"

2"

1"X 4"X 10"

7/8"X 2½" Slots

1" Holes ½" deep

Wheels
3/4"X 2"
(4) Reqd.

Helmets
(4) Reqd.

## POOR MAN'S MINI BEADING PLANE

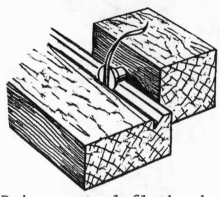

Drive a steel flathead wood screw into a scrap wood block. The groove in the steel screw head acts as a mini cutter. The width of the cut bead is controlled by simply turning the screw in or out. Look out, Black & Decker!

Then, after twenty years we cash in our food stamps and buy 8,000 shares of IBM.

## TINY TOTS TOTER

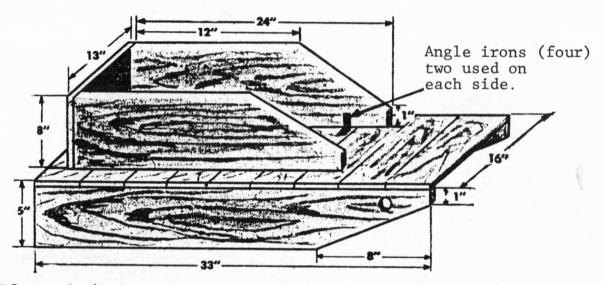

Angle irons (four) two used on each side.

If you don't have any tiny tots to tote around on this little sled, then try packages, groceries, firewood, or anything else that you folks in snow country might need to tote by sled. Use scrap 3/4" pine lumber with 1½" aluminum wood screws to build. Do not use plywood if you can avoid it. Finish with either stain and varnish, or paint. Tie a strong rope to the holes in front. Just think, build this right and you get to haul kids around on the next bitter cold, snowy day. How come you're so lucky?

DOWEL DOLLS

One of the greatest things about children is their gift of an active imagination. Give a child a stick and it becomes a gun. A cardboard box can be transformed into a ten-room house. A pencil turns into a supersonic jet airplane. All it takes is imagination. And so it is with these little Dowel Dolls. They certainly aren't the most beautiful dolls around, but for the right child they can become a prince and his princess on their way to the grand ball. For very small children, glue all the parts together so they won't be tempted to taste-test the parts. For older children, leave the parts loose so they can take them apart and put them together again. Finish by sanding and decorating with non-toxic paints. Use your imagination!

DOLLS SHOWN ACTUAL SIZE
1. Cut all dowel parts to size.
2. Drill all holes for parts. All holes are ¼" deep.
3. Sand all parts.
4. Paint and assemble.

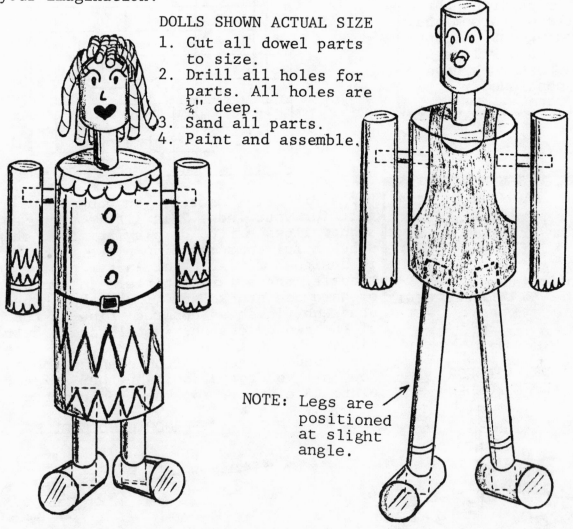

NOTE: Legs are positioned at slight angle.

HEAD: ½" X 3/4" dowel
HAIR: knitting yarn held with glue
BODY: 1 1/8" X 2½" dowel
NECK: ¼" X 3/4" dowel
ARMS: 3/8" X 1½" dowel
ARM PINS: 1/8" X 5/8" dowel
LEGS: ¼" X 1" dowel
FEET 3/8" X 1" dowel

HEAD: ½" X 3/4" dowel
NOSE & EARS: 1/8" dowel ears sanded
BODY: 1 1/8" X 3/4" dowel
NECK: ¼" X 3/4" dowel
ARMS: 3/8" X 1 3/4" dowel
ARM PINS: 1/8" X 5/8" dowel
LEGS: ¼" X 2¼" dowel
FEET: 3/8" X 1" dowel

## DECORATOR'S LAW

After papering three walls of a room and running out of paper, the store will tell you that they have discontinued your pattern.

## PLATE HOLDER

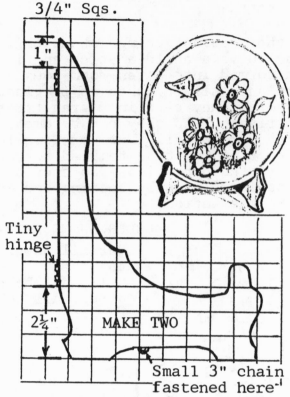

3/4" Sqs.

1"

Tiny hinge

2¼"   MAKE TWO

Small 3" chain fastened here

## MAGICIANS

are persons who with prices, taxes, and inflation going up, can live within their income.

Using 3/8" or ¼" stock, you can make a nice gift for your lady. This little plate holder stand allows her to display her fine china or a beautiful commemorative plate. This holder is designed for a 10" or larger plate. Just transfer the enlarged pattern to two pieces of hardwood stock, and jigsaw the shapes. Sand and finish as desired. Line up the backs of the two pieces and install small butt hinges. Mount a small link 3" chain beneath the stand to keep it from opening too far. Now, all you gotta do is buy her a fancy plate to display. You know you can't win!

## DRILL PRESS WORK HOLDER

One way to hold wood or other material steady on a drill press table, is to glue two sheets of sandpaper back to back. This forms a nonskid insert between work and table.

## BROOM HANDLE FILE

The cut-off end of an old broom handle makes a great handle for a file. However, don't make the mistake of asking your wife where she hides her old brooms. This sorta implies she's a witch. And you're liable to end up eating three feet of broom handle! I know!!!

SURE-GRIP BENCH STOP

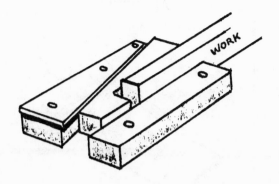

Designed especially for holding wood for planing, we have found a number of other uses for this little bench stop.

It will hold a board upright, by the edge, for carving, sanding, and even painting. It will serve as a glue clamp, nailing clamp, and saw clamp. It will clamp and hold parts at an angle for special finishing. Matter-of-fact, there isn't much we haven't used it for. It makes a perfect "third" hand when you need one most.

Since both jaws are always parallel, it has a very tight grip, but won't mar soft woods. It is designed for gripping boards of various thicknesses as they are pushed in, yet it will release immediately when the work is pulled back. A time saver when you're in a hurry.

This simple little clamp should be made from 3/4" hardwood, except the top guide which is ¼" plywood. It is important that at least the wedge be made from hardwood, as it does take a beating over a period of time. Use only heavy wood screws to attach the parts to your work bench. Nails just won't hold up under heavy use. You will be amazed at how something this simple to build can be so useful in your shop. And since it can be made from wood scraps, the cost is right!

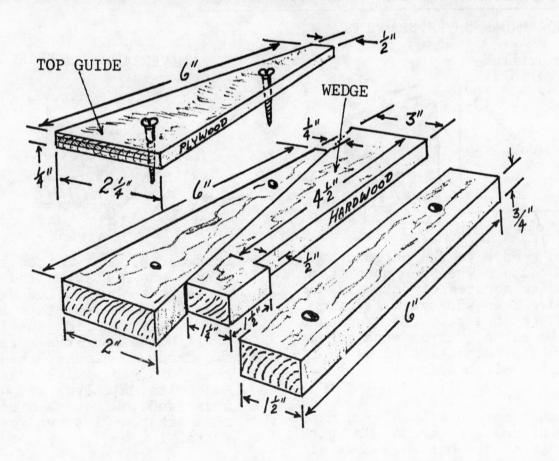

142

# Position Wanted

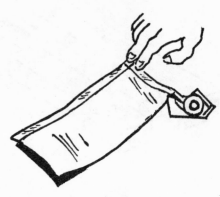

While we know that you will instantly recognize him from his famous Pepsodent smile and starring movie roles, Mr. Cheeta Kong is now free to offer his services. Having outgrown his movie roles as Tarzan's sidekick, he comes with excellent recommendations from the Friendly Finance Company where he served as Vice President in charge of terminal collections. He is a graduate of Harvard Banana School where he is fondly remembered by the local Police Department as the protest leader of BKTAOE (Be Kind to Apes--Or Else!). He earned his Ph.D. in Mayhem while employed part time with MALFIA Corp., where he rose through the ranks with unusual speed due to the sudden demise (or early retirement) of each of his supervisors. Known to one and all as "Mr. Personality," Mr. Kong is now ready to serve you. He is a firm believer in the old axiom "There is only one way to do things--his!"

Contact:
TARZAN'S PERSONNEL SERVICES, Kenya, W. Africa

## TEAR PREVENTER

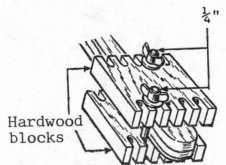

A sheet of sandpaper has a bad tendency to tear when clamped to the shoe of an orbital sander. Just a small tear will slacken the tension on the paper and keep it from moving with the shoe. Prevent this by reinforcing all edges with masking tape as shown. Your sandpaper will both work harder and last longer.

## POOR MAN'S SHELF BRACKETS

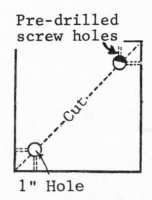
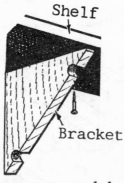

You don't have to run out and buy shelf brackets when you need them. Just a few squares of scrap lumber that have been squared will give you all the brackets that you need. Drill 1" holes 2" from each corner to permit placement of screws. Drill four holes slightly smaller than the screws that you will be using in the edgeso of the square as shown. Then saw each square diagonally to make a pair of shelf brackets. Oh, eat your hearts out, hardware makers!

## UNIVERSAL GLUE CLAMP

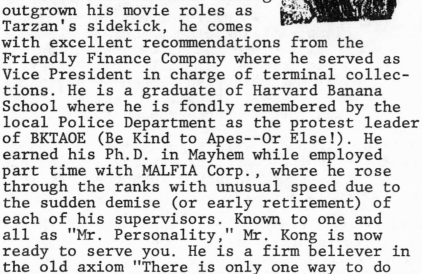

Hardwood blocks slotted in the manner shown above allow great pressure to be applied evenly over a glued area. This makes for a tight, solid glue joint. Drill holes near the edges of two hardwood blocks, then open them into slots with a saw. Add bolts, washers, and wing-nuts, and you have a nice glue clamp that will serve you for years.

## C-CLAMP VISE

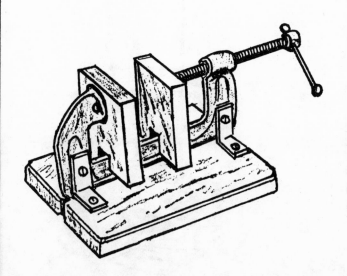

Many times the woodworker will find that his heavy-duty shop vise just won't do for clamping delicate parts. The heavy metal jaws can scratch or damage woodwork. If doing light soldering work, the heavy metal jaws draw heat away from the work. Sometimes a light-duty vise with soft jaws can do the job much better.

You can easily and inexpensively build such a vise from an old C-clamp and some hardwood scraps. Use at least a 3" clamp, and one made by steel stamping rather than cast-iron if possible.

Cut two hardwood blocks to size for the frame. Attach these blocks to the C-clamp firmly, using right-angle shelf brackets. To provide a large, soft gripping surface, fit wooden pads to each jaw of the clamp. Fasten one pad with countersunk machine screws at the top of the "C". For the screw side pad, drill an undersized hole, then press the pad over the round foot of the clamp screw. Notch the bottoms of both wood pads to fit over the C-clamp frame. You can screw, or clamp, this vise to your workbench top. It makes a great little glue clamp for small parts and is perfect for delicate craft or hobby work.

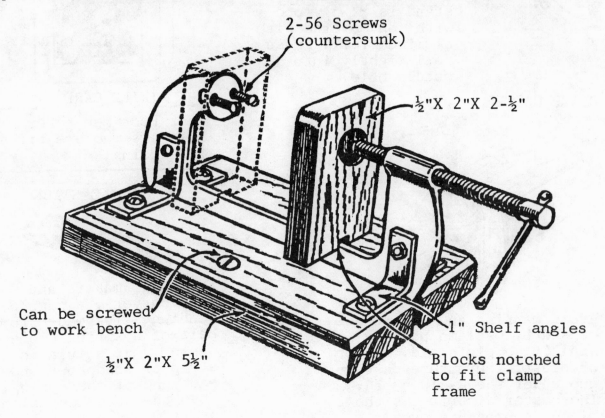

2-56 Screws (countersunk)

½"X 2"X 2-½"

Can be screwed to work bench

½"X 2"X 5½"

1" Shelf angles

Blocks notched to fit clamp frame

## HURRICANE LAMP

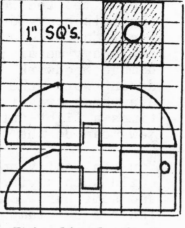

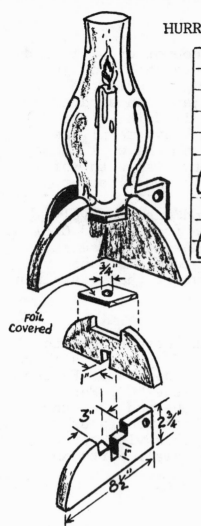

Foil
Covered

This little lamp can brighten someone's day, or night. Makes a great table centerpiece. And, it's easier to build than it looks. Build from 3/4" stock. Buy a lamp chimney and insert over candle on stand. Base can be painted and decorated. The candle holder stand is ¼" plywood with top covered with aluminum foil. Press foil tightly into candle hole.

## CLAMP CASTER

Avoid marring and indentions caused by C-clamp pads by installing a plain old, rubber or plastic furniture caster cup under the C-clamp pad. The caster distributes the clamping pressure over a much greater area.

WILD CARD

For Poor Man poker players who are tired of losing!

## SANDING STICK

For model makers and wood carvers, a simple sanding stick made from half of a spring clothespin. Just slip a thin strip of sandpaper under each end of the spring. Move the sandpaper along as it wears out at the end.

# POOR MAN'S MINI PLANE

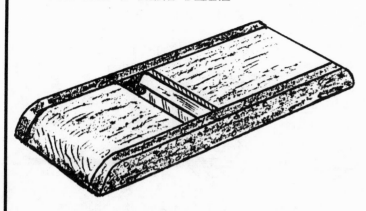

Nowadays, the price of a good wood plane can easily run as much as some power tools. And it's a tool most wood craftsmen wouldn't be without. May we present the Poor Man's Mini Plane. Not as fancy as its commercial brothers, but a whole lot easier on the pocketbook.

It can be built from shop scraps and uses old single or double edge razor blades as plane blades. After shaving your face they can be put to work shaving wood. They stay sharp for a long time, but when they do get dull are cheap and easy to replace. Something that can't be said for most commercial models.

The size of our mini model is only about 6" but can be varied to suit if desired. Use only hardwood strips for the sides and attach to the body with glue and 1" brads as shown. The width of the plane is determined by the width of the razor blade used. The blade is held in position by two small wood screws (one on each side of the razor blade). Allow a 1/16" slot for the blade to protrude across the bottom.

While our Mini Plane is limited to light duty and fine cuts, it does a beautiful job. Finish by rubbing down both top and bottom with wax. And the price is right! What more can a Poor Man ask? Look out Monkey Wards!

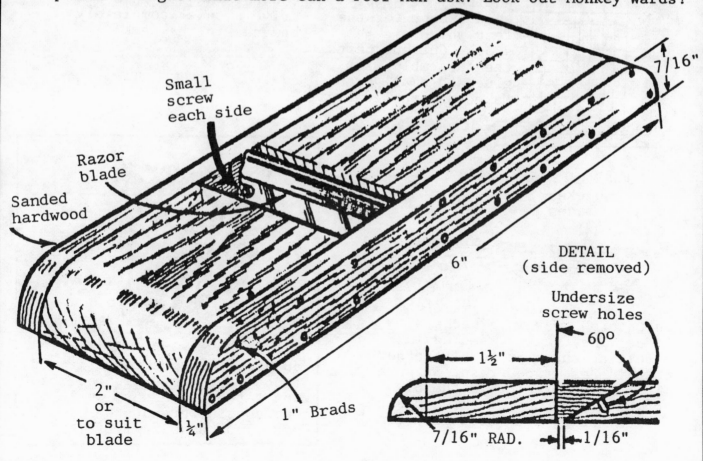

Small screw each side

Razor blade

Sanded hardwood

7/16"

6"

DETAIL (side removed)

Undersize screw holes

60°

1½"

2" or to suit blade

¼"

1" Brads

7/16" RAD.

1/16"

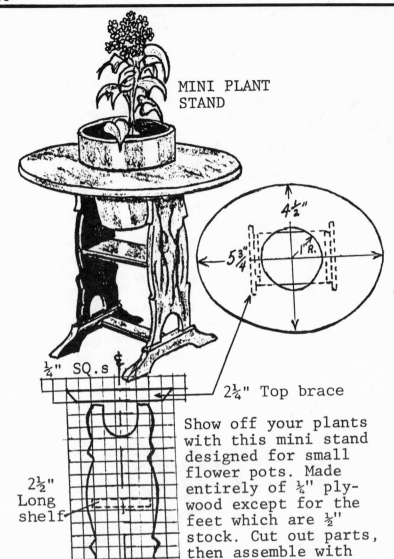

MINI PLANT STAND

4½"

5¾"

1" R.

¼" SQ.s

2¼" Top brace

2½" Long shelf

½" stock foot

Bottom brace 2½" long

Show off your plants with this mini stand designed for small flower pots. Made entirely of ¼" plywood except for the feet which are ½" stock. Cut out parts, then assemble with glue and small brads. Makes an excellent gift.

## WOOD SCREW LOCK

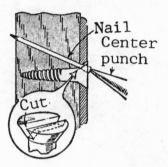

Nail
Center
punch

Cut

If you really want to harass a thief, try this little stunt. Hinges and hasps can be made most difficult to remove from doors, tool chests, storage sheds, etc., if the screws holding them are locked so that a screwdriver can't remove them. Simply deepen the screw slot at an acute angle at one end. Turn the screw tightly in place, then drive a finishing nail into the slot so that the head is below the surface. Use a center punch to countersink it. This will drive a thief completely bananas in the dark!

## POOR MAN'S WOOD RASP

Hacksaw blades

Stove bolts

Formed handle

Don't throw away worn hacksaw blades. They can be used again by bolting three or four together and using as a wood rasp. Be sure all teeth are facing in the direction of cut, then bend a piece of light strap iron to form a handle.

## SAY IT ISN'T SO!

You didn't forget to get a copy of the Poor Man's Catalog for your father, brother, uncle, son, cousin, grandfather, or boss. Your boss's girlfriend?

## POOR MAN'S SANDERS

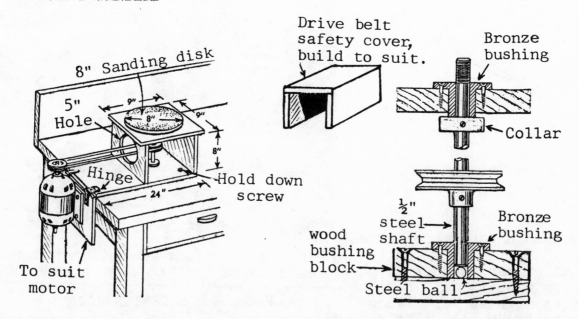

Here is a collection of sanders that can all be built from shop scraps. The little horizontal, power disk sander is built as a portable unit. It can be removed from your workbench and stored by the removal of the hold-down screw. Note that this unit is built in two separate pieces. The motor mounting board is hinged to fold over the side of your workbench. The weight of the motor keeps the drive belt tight. A fairly low-speed motor of 1400 rpm (or less) should be used. The ½" steel shaft rests on a steel ball bearing. The lower bronze bushing should be set in a wooden block so that the ball bearing rests directly on the surface of the sander base. Build the base, disk table, and motor mounting board of 3/4" stock. We suggest that you also build a three-sided box as a safety cover over the drive belt. It can be mounted permanently to the base with wood screws driven upwards through the bottom of the base.

The two sanding blocks are built from scrap and use wedges to hold paper.

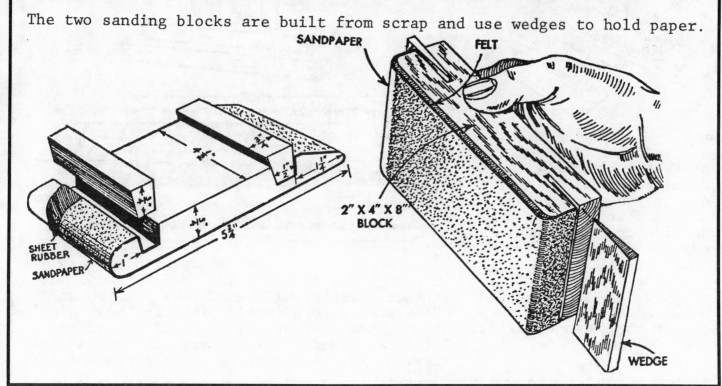

## FLOOR STRAIGHTENER

Actually, this doesn't straighten floors. But it will help you to fit a panel or hang a door even with an irregular floor. This job is almost as much fun as trying to tile a bathroom wall that's 15° out of plumb. Just tape a pencil to a piece of scrap wood and slide across the floor, tracing the exact pattern of the floor. Cut on the traced line.

## SELF-LOCKING MINI SANDER

A 3" section of plastic hose or tubing makes an excellent self-locking, contour sander. Just make a slit down the center and insert one edge of the sandpaper into the slit. Then wrap the paper around the hose and insert the other edge. Hand pressure clamps the paper securely.

Man, that restaurant was so bad, the roast turkey got up and walked out!

## POOR MAN'S CENTERPIECE

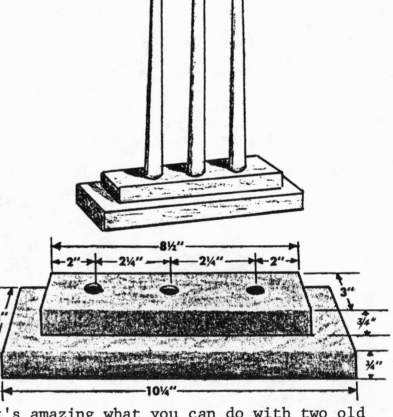

It's amazing what you can do with two old scrap pieces of wood. Cut, drill, sand, and attach together with wood screws as shown. Decorated with nature's pine branches, pine cones, holly, flowers, or fruit in season, it makes a beautiful centerpiece for any occasion. And you gotta admit, the cost is AOK.

# POOR MAN'S TABLE SAW

A good stationary table saw will cost you a bundle nowadays. But a good, bolt-down table saw converted from your portable electric saw is even better. It gives you both a portable saw when you need one, and a table saw for precision, heavy-duty sawing. You get the best of two worlds, and the cost is just right--cheap!

Use 3/4" plywood to build the table. A metal plate is rabbeted flush into the top. The base plate of your portable saw is clamped against the metal plate. One edge of the base plate is held by a stationary block, the other by a sliding block locked by a wing nut as shown in the drawing. The length and width measurements are not given for the metal plate as you must fit to size your own portable saw. The blade slot cut into the metal plate must be large enough to allow the telescoping guard on your saw to emerge through the slot. Make sure the guard works easily. For simple operation, install a plug-in receptacle, with switch, on the saw table into which you can plug the saw cord.

Build the rip fence as shown, making the clamping mechanism from a 4" mending plate sawed into 2¼" and 1 3/4" pieces. Notch the short piece into the near end of rip fence and attach with two lag screws. Drill and tap the long piece near the bottom for a wing screw. This wing screw bears against the short metal piece exerting pressure when tightened.

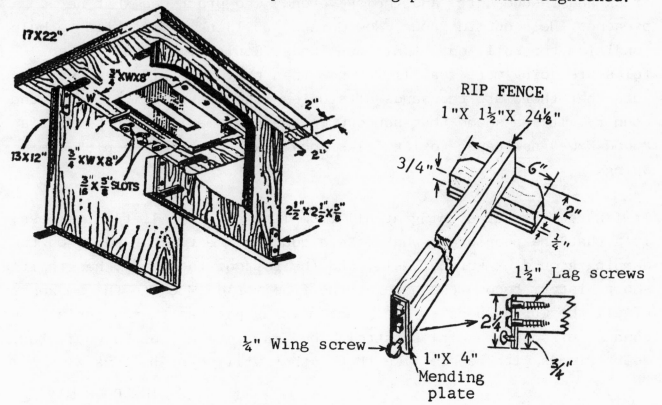

RIP FENCE

## PROFILES

One of the most interesting things about being in the mail order business is the number of "Real People" that you get to meet--even if only
through the mail. There are many thousands of folks out there doing
their own thing--working folks who are busy creating new lives for
themselves and their families. And anyone who says that retired folks
are over the hill when it comes to "doing" had better take a second
look. We have hundreds of "retired" customers who are busier than a
cat in a rain barrel filled with mice. Like the retired naval officer
in a large city who spends all his spare time teaching young school
"drop outs" how to read and write. Or the old gentleman in Oregon
known as Chief Tellumhow. He teaches young Indian children the almost
forgotten art of arrowhead making as it was practiced by their ancest-
ors many years ago. And my friend the "flying dentist" who retired,
only to spend most of his time down in South America using his skills
to treat people so desperately poor that they can't afford the rags
on their backs. And I can't forget my favorite all-volunteer fire/
rescue unit (all retirees during the day) in a small town bordering
a large interstate highway. They were credited with saving six lives
last year. They also raised the money to buy the town's only fire-
truck and rescue unit. And the "Reverend" who practices what he
preaches. He's out in Papua, New Guinea, building a lime kiln to help
condition the soil, out of his own funds. Retired, my foot! These
folks are doing more real living now than they ever did. I'm quite
sure that there are thousands of stories like these from all over the
country. It's a shame that someone in the news media dosen't start a
"Good News" newspaper to let folks know what the "Real People" are
doing.

If I have learned anything at all from life and this little business,
it's that the people are what make a country great. What was once the
dumping ground of Europe, Asia, and the rest of the world, has in it's
short history become the hope of the free world. Much to the amazement
of all the worlds people, the great melting pot has turned out a
country of solid, stainless steel. They may love us, or hate us, but,
dear friends, with people like these, they will never beat us.

THE POOR MAN

POOR MAN'S BOOMERANG

On the following few pages you will learn a little about the world's oldest sport--the making and throwing of boomerangs. And you will learn from an expert. I had made a few, and even sold a few, a number of years ago. I enjoyed it so much that I wrote a booklet on it which appears in our u-build catalog. But I always treated it as more of a hobby than anything else. From Rusty Harding, I learned that it's a lot more than a hobby; it's a real craft. A very popular craft. Once a year the Smithsonian Institution in Washington, D.C., holds a week-long boomerang meet with thousands of folks from around the world attending. They hold all types of boomerang competitions from the longest flight, to the smallest boomerang. They have classes and lectures given by the leading experts in the field. In short, they have a ball!

Rusty Harding builds, flies, designs, and markets boomerangs. He is a retired aerospace engineer specializing in flight-control systems for aircraft and spacecraft. He retired early and moved to Florida, where he and his family build some of the best boomerangs in the world. His boomerangs are marketed worldwide. Each is handmade and carefully tested before it can be sold. When Rusty heard that we were doing this book, he sent me a very special boomerang which I prize greatly. He designed and named this boomerang the "Poor Man's Boomerang" especially for the readers of this book. If you have any questions about boomerangs, or would like to purchase one or more, contact him: Rusty Harding, Boomerangs, P.O. Box 2884, Vero Beach, FL 32960. Rusty gives the following instructions for building your own Poor Man's Boomerang:
**********************************************************************

BOOMERANG CONSTRUCTION

The art of boomerang throwing is probably the world's oldest sport, yet few people have seen one thrown properly, and fewer still have thrown one themselves. These instructions will allow you to make your own boomerang from $\frac{1}{4}$" plywood. With a little care, your boomerang should return to you when thrown properly, providing hours of fun in this fascinating sport.

Use the best $\frac{1}{4}$", 5-ply plywood that you can get. Make a cardboard pattern of the boomerang, following the layout. Posterboard works well for this. Before you trace the pattern on the plywood, decide what kind of saw you will cut your boomerang blank out with. Trace the pattern on the wood so that the rough edge of the saw cut will be on the top of the boomerang where it will be removed later in shaping. Coping saws, jig saws, and band saws leave a rough edge on the lower surface, whereas sabre saws leave the rough edge on the upper surface. Spend a little time planning. It will be to your advantage! Choose a piece of plywood that is relatively flat. If it does have a slight curve or warp, be sure that the concave side is used for the top of your finished boomerang. A boomerang with a convex top WILL NOT WORK! Cut out the boomerang. Don't worry about the rough edges at this point as most will disappear during shaping.

On the cut out blank, draw guide lines for the bevels using the dimensions shown on the shaping layout. Take care to note leading/trailing edges. Note that these instructions are for a right-handed boomerang. Lefties should make a mirror image of this one for throwing with the

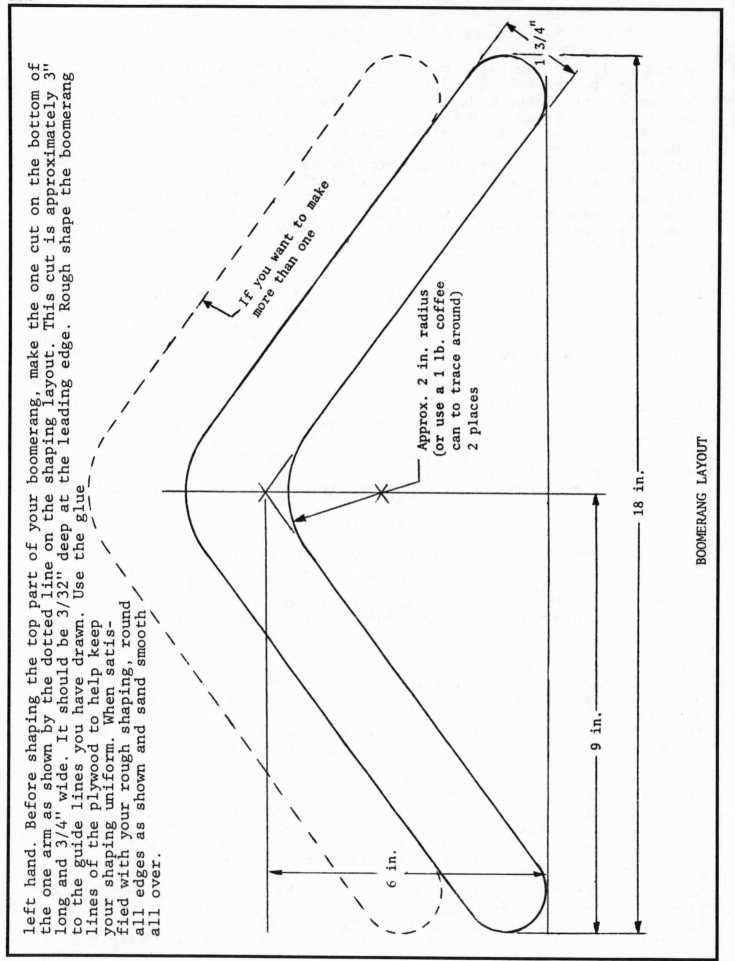

left hand. Before shaping the top part of your boomerang, make the one cut on the bottom of the one arm as shown by the dotted line on the shaping layout. This cut is approximately 3" long and 3/4" wide. It should be 3/32" deep at the leading edge. Rough shape the boomerang to the guide lines you have drawn. Use the glue lines of the plywood to help keep your shaping uniform. When satisfied with your rough shaping, round all edges as shown and sand smooth all over.

If you want to make more than one

Approx. 2 in. radius (or use a 1 lb. coffee can to trace around) 2 places

1 3/4"

18 in.

9 in.

6 in.

BOOMERANG LAYOUT

153

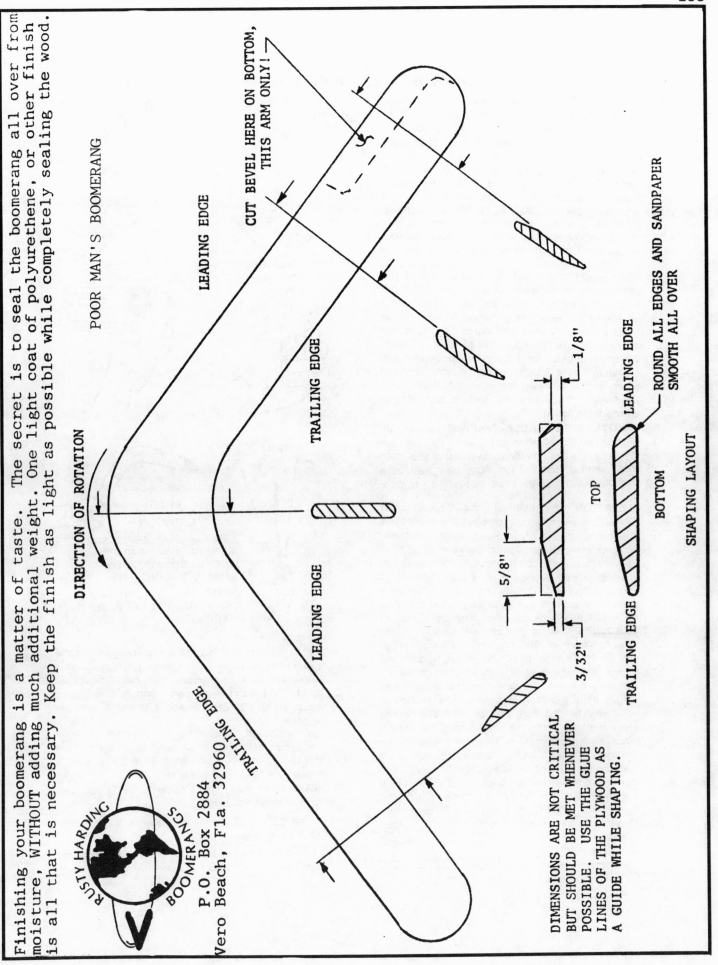

Finishing your boomerang is a matter of taste. The secret is to seal the boomerang all over from moisture, WITHOUT adding much additional weight. One light coat of polyurethene, or other finish is all that is necessary. Keep the finish as light as possible while completely sealing the wood.

POOR MAN'S BOOMERANG

DIRECTION OF ROTATION

LEADING EDGE

TRAILING EDGE

LEADING EDGE

TRAILING EDGE

CUT BEVEL HERE ON BOTTOM, THIS ARM ONLY!

RUSTY HARDING
BOOMERANGS
P.O. Box 2884
Vero Beach, Fla. 32960

1/8"

5/8"

3/32"

TOP

LEADING EDGE

BOTTOM

TRAILING EDGE

SHAPING LAYOUT

ROUND ALL EDGES AND SANDPAPER SMOOTH ALL OVER

DIMENSIONS ARE NOT CRITICAL BUT SHOULD BE MET WHENEVER POSSIBLE. USE THE GLUE LINES OF THE PLYWOOD AS A GUIDE WHILE SHAPING.

## THROWING YOUR BOOMERANG

Learning to throw a quality handcrafted returning Boomerang is not difficult. However, you should spend a few minutes learning the correct method in order to get satisfactory returns. Boomerangs are right handed and left handed. These instructions are written for the right handed thrower. Left handers using a left handed Boomerang should simply substitute left for right and right for left wherever they appear in these instructions.

**STANCE -** Stand comfortably with the wind striking your left cheek, so that you are facing approximately 45° to the right of the direction the wind is coming from. *See Figure 1.*

**GRIP —** With the flat (or back) side of the Boomerang in the palm of your hand, grip the Boomerang as in *Figure 2.* No more than 1½ to 2 inches of the Boomerang should be held in the hand, as more will keep you from putting the proper amount of spin on the Boomerang when it is thrown. Wrap one or two fingers around the Boomerang as shown in Figure 3. Stronger persons may prefer to pinch the Boomerang between the thumb and forefinger. *See Figure 4.* Use the grip that is comfortable for you.

**LAYOVER or TILT ANGLE -** The Boomerang should be nearly vertical when launched. Typically, the layover angle should vary from vertical to about 30° from vertical. Each Boomerang flies best at a particular layover angle so adjust to suit. *See Figure 5.*

**ELEVATION -** The Boomerang should be launched on a slight upward flight path, 5 to 15° upward from horizontal. To do this, face in the throwing direction, and pick a target 40 to 50 yards away and about 15 to 20 feet above the ground. Aim at a distant object or an imaginary point in space, but always think of it as your aiming point. The idea here is to establish a point, then change it as necessary to get accurate returns. This will be explained later. *See Figure 6.*

**THROWING -** Bring your arm and the Boomerang straight back over your shoulder, and, keeping your eye on the aiming point, throw the Boomerang toward the aiming point with an overarm swing, stopping the arm suddenly just about shoulder height as the arm is extended. The motion is somewhat like cracking a whip. The Boomerang should snap out of your hand toward the aiming point, spinning rapidly in a vertical plane. As the Boomerang goes outward, it should be thrown with just enough power to cause it to return to you. If it does not come all the way back to you, throw a little harder, but if it travels past you on return, you have probably thrown it too hard. Adjust your throwing power for complete returns.

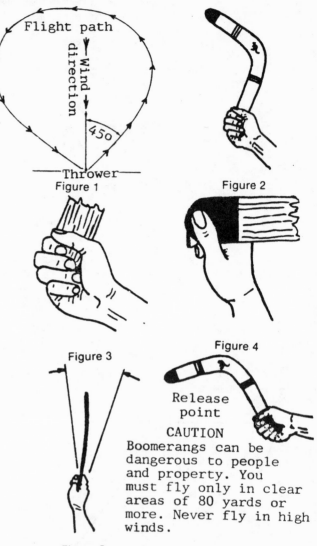

Figure 1

Figure 2

Figure 3

Figure 4

Release point

CAUTION
Boomerangs can be dangerous to people and property. You must fly only in clear areas of 80 yards or more. Never fly in high winds.

Figure 5

Get sufficient spin on the Boomerang. While the exact amount of spin is not critical, having enough is important as a Boomerang with insufficient spin **WILL NOT FLY!** A properly thrown Boomerang spins about 600 RPM or about 10 revolutions per second.

Be consistent! Consistency is important, because until you can throw the same way each time, you will not know what you are doing wrong, and will not know how to correct the error.

If the Boomerang lands consistently to your left, turn more to your right.

If the Boomerang lands consistently to your right, turn more to your left.

If the Boomerang lands consistently in front of you, aim your throw a little higher or throw a little harder.

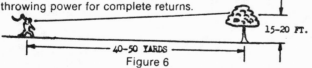

15-20 FT.

40-50 YARDS

Figure 6

# For the Rich Man

Following in the tradition set by our Poor Man's Catalogs #3 and #4, of trying to have something for everyone, we were hard put to come up with something worthy of the rich man in this book. After all, inflation, a recession, and the IRS tend to have bad financial effects on the rich, too. Let's face it, they have more to lose. As the Hunt brothers said "All clouds don't have silver linings!" Things are tough all over. Consider that poor stock broker who specialized only in Chrysler stocks. He had to trade his Mercedes in on a Japanese Cadillac (Honda).

With such trying times for the rich, we had to call in our staff of marketing experts--two astrologers, three witch doctors, one unemployed politician, and our plumber's summer replacement, David Rockefeller. We felt that we needed someone with big money experience, and tried to get Johnny Carson--but he was on vacation. After lengthy consultation, from which some very good (but unprintable) suggestions were turned down, it was decided to give our rich coupon clippers the following big break:

34¢ OFF 34¢

ROLLS ROYCE

POOR MAN

Sorry, only one per family at these prices

SILVER WRAITH II

**ON YOUR NEXT ROLLS ROYCE**

# INDEX OF PROJECTS AND STORIES

## Sports

## Woodworking

## POOR MAN'S CONTEST

ATTENTION: All you poor men (and poor women)!
Here's your big chance to get published!

If you send us an original, usable, money-saving plan or idea;
and if we use it in our next catalog, we'll acknowledge your
contribution and send you a FREE copy of The Poor Man's
Catalog #5. (This is our own self-published catalog and not
the catalog you're holding in your hands.)

Send your ideas and plans to:

POOR MAN'S CONTEST
Poor Man's Catalog
Post Office Box 23
Highland, Maryland 20777

No purchase is necessary to qualify. Just send your original ideas.
If they are used in forthcoming catalogs you will be notified and
acknowledged in the catalog. Submission of ideas or plans by readers
constitutes your permission of accepted ideas or plans to be published
in any forthcoming Poor Man's catalog. Submissions will not be
returned or acknowledged. If winner has already purchased our catalog
#5, we will send refund.